Bible Studies for Small Groups

by Lyman Coleman

British Editors: Anton Baumohl, Lance Pierson, Emlyn Williams, and Peter Price

SCRIPTURE UNION
130 City Road, London EC1V 2NJ

© 1983 Serendipity House

UK Edition © Scripture Union 1985

Published by Scripture Union,
130 City Road, London EC1V 2NJ

ISBN 0 86201 319 4

Printed in Great Britain by
Ebenezer Baylis & Son Limited,
The Trinity Press, Worcester and London.

CONTENTS

This leader's guide gives you all the tools you need to introduce Serendipity to your church – either into existing groups or when forming new groups. This guide is intended for leaders only; the study courses *Basics* and *I Believe* are available as separate publications for group members.

We recommend that before leading groups, using this method, leaders attend a training course or go through the Training Programme at the beginning of this manual.

SERENDIPITY BIBLE STUDIES FOR HOME GROUPS
A guide to the units in this series

BEGINNER UNITS	WEEKS	GOAL	STUDY METHOD	GROUP COVENANT
Basics	6	To get aquainted, and share your "God stories"	Relational—to share your "story" through "the Story" of Scripture	In the first two units you agree to: (1) meet once a week (2) share your "God story" (3) hold everything that is said in confidence (4) hold each other accountable (5) call on one another when you're down (6) reach out to others who are lonely
I Believe	6	To examine what you believe on the Apostles' Creed	Self inventory—to identify where you stand on critical areas of faith	

Both books are incorporated into this Leader's Guide.

ADVANCED UNITS	WEEKS	GOAL	STUDY METHOD	GROUP COVENANT
Epistles	11	To learn how to study the Letters of the N.T.	Basic Inductive—to examine *Ephesians*—paragraph by paragraph, completing a worksheet as you go	In the advanced units, you agree (in addition to the 6 disciplines above) to: (7) complete the Bible study assignment BEFORE the group meeting (8) share the leadership, rotating around the group (9) hold a monthly fun social for your children, friends and family
Gospels				
Psalms				
Old Testament	6	To learn how to study any O.T. historical book	Historical narrative—to trace the "story" of salvation in the "story" of Scripture	

Advanced units are gradually being replaced with new British material (Serendipity Discipleship series) and we regret that when present stocks are exhausted no further copies will be available.

For details of the new series please contact your supplier or Scripture Union.

INTRODUCTION TO SERENDIPITY

Serendipity group Bible study books
Serendipity: 'making unexpected discoveries'

As a word it isn't new, in fact it has been around since the 18th Century. As a method of group Bible study, however, it is new. Serendipity Bible study material was originally developed in the United States by Lyman Coleman and was tested and refined over a number of years in churches of different denominations across America. In 1983 Scripture Union, perceiving a growing need in British churches, took Lyman's material and produced British editions.

This leader's guide forms an introductory course for all those wishing to use the Serendipity approach in their house group or adult Bible study group.

What is the Serendipity approach?
Serendipity Bible study is essentially a course for small groups, and centres around the growth of relationships in such groups that meet to study the Bible. It's an approach that helps groups to discover the true meaning of *Koinonia* – a fellowship where people really care and support one another. In each study emphasis is placed on encouraging people to apply God's word in a way that produces action and change and in an atmosphere where there is trust, encouragement and support. In such groups pastoral care develops as a natural consequence of learning together.

An Understanding of groups
Central to the Serendipity approach is an understanding of how relationships can be nurtured in small groups so that people can learn to take risks in opening themselves to God and to each other. This understanding is best represented by the diamond diagram below. Each point of the diamond represents a stage in the life of the group.

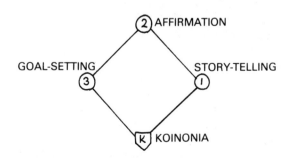

People need the opportunity to share something of themselves and need to hear others sharing elements of their own lives before relationships begin to open up – this has been called *Storytelling*. Everyone needs to know that they are being listened to and need encouragement in their learning and in their relationships. We are to respond with a 'thank you' or 'I found your contribution helpful' etc. In the diamond this is called, *Affirmation*. In experiencing these things in a group that meets together on a regular basis (even over a limited number of weeks) people begin to share their deeper longings or hurts, or discover that they can trust others to support them in their struggles. Individuals begin to share what God is saying to them and the changes they need to make in the way they live. This is called *Goal-setting*. Serendipity Bible study material encourages these stages to be reached through Bible study. If you want to know more about the diamond refer to Session 2 in the training course, enclosed in this leader's guide.

Needs in our churches
The needs addressed by this material are reflected in our churches and in society:

The need for applied biblical knowledge: Christians are crying out for help in applying their Christian faith in an increasingly complex world. *Knowing* the Bible isn't enough – people want to know how to translate this knowledge into action.

The need to belong: the increased pace of living, the constant moving of home, people's general business – all work against the development of deep relationships. Many feel the need for relationships that are more satisfying, long-lasting with greater commitment and depth of caring. Some long to belong to a group where there is some stability. Some feel that deeper relationships should be a distinctive feature of the local church as it witnesses to a lonely generation.

Sharing the burden: pressures on Christians as they try to survive in the world are often intolerable – witnessed by emotional/psychological disorders, increased divorce and the problems of parenting. Many feel that one answer to this is for Christians to share each others' burdens more seriously – not just prayerfully but in practical ways as well.

The church as a community: a growing conviction that the church is meant to be a community of Christians of all ages and backgrounds who demonstrate in the way they live the true nature of God's Kindgom and who experience what the New Testament means by *Koinonia* or fellowship.

A guide to this series

This book contains all you should need to introduce Serendipity to your church and if you have never used this type of material before we recommend that you go through this leader's guide thoroughly – even if you hope to use the material with existing church groups.

In this leader's guide you will find:

An introduction to Serendipity: you've been reading it and you should now know something about the special approach.

How to run a Serendipity group: practical notes for leaders of groups.

Leader's Training Programme: even if you have been leading groups for twenty-five years we recommend you put yourself through a training course that orientates you to the Serendipity method. If you can attend a course being run in your locality – great! If there isn't one you could write to Scripture Union or Serendipity UK and ask if it's possible to organise one. If that fails, get a few people together and run your own course using the six-session training programme included in this leader's guide. It will help you to understand the theory and the practice!

Basics: this is a six-week Bible study course on some of the basics of the Christian life, ideal for a new group or one new to Serendipity. It can be purchased as a separate booklet so that each member of your Bible Study group can have a copy (from Christian bookshops or direct from Scripture Union Mail Order, 9-11 Clothier Road, Brislington, Bristol, BS4 5RL).

I Believe: A six week Bible study course on the major beliefs of Christians as stated in the Apostles' Creed. Again ideal for new groups or groups new to Serendipity or for groups studying Christian basics. You may choose between *Basics* and *I Believe* or decide to study both. (*I Believe* is also available as a separate booklet).

Families Programme: There is always a danger that small groups become inward-looking and closed to outsiders. To encourage openness a collection of ideas for lighter, open meetings are incorporated in the last section entitled *Families*. Serendipity groups are encouraged to regularly open their doors to friends, neighbours and children and to share some of the fun of being together with them.

The *Introduction, Training Programme* and *Families' Programme* are only available in this leader's guide.

Other studies

Four other studies are also available in this series for adult groups and details of these books are printed on page 4. These studies provide a taste of different methods of study with more emphasis on understanding the Bible passage through analysis and paraphrase. Your groups may like to choose one of these studies for a change or may prefer to go to a different Serendipity series.

Serendipity UK

In 1984 Serendipity UK was formed to produce a further Serendipity Bible Study series designed specifically for British churches. If you are interested in receiving details of these contact Scripture Union who continue to act as publishers for the new material.

HOW TO RUN A SERENDIPITY GROUP

Using Serendipity to form new groups

Serendipity is essentially group study material and to be used effectively requires the establishment of small groups of people committed to meeting regularly at least for the duration of the course (six sessions).

Groups of between five and twelve people are ideal for these studies – meeting in people's homes or in a hall. Where groups are larger we recommend that they are sub-divided, each sub. group with its own trained leader. Two or more groups could work independently in the same hall in this way.

New people can join groups after a series has been started but care must be taken to incorporate them into an existing group. The leader should meet the newcomer beforehand, if possible, to explain what has happened so far. Time can be given at the beginning of the session for the newcomer to introduce themselves to the other members and vice versa.

We strongly recommend the use of an agreement where members of the group commit themselves to each other for the duration of the course. At the beginning of *Basics* and *I Believe* a group covenant is set out for participants to sign.

Using Serendipity in established groups

We would suggest that any group – however long it's been going and however well people know each other – that has never used Serendipity before should try *Basics* or *I Believe* before any of the other units, and that leaders should be trained in this new type of Bible study. Because the method is different to many other types of group Bible study you will need to prepare group members for something different – a different way of asking questions, different type of discussion, different emphasis (application rather than just understanding). Anyone used to a particular form of study is liable to resist something new, but gently persevere and encourage everyone to participate.

Our experience shows that established groups gain far more than they expect to, when they use the programme in full. Among the gains for existing groups are: even deeper relationships, the chance for everyone to think and speak, the assistance to leaders in helping them to handle the group – its silences, the shy members and the dominant ones.

Leading a group

Leadership of a small group should not be taken on lightly. Each small group needs a leader who understands Serendipity material, has time to prepare beforehand, takes responsibility for seeing that people remember group times etc. If possible, leaders should attend a Serendipity training course or at least use the training course available in this book. Details of training events are available from: Scripture Union Training Unit, 9-11 Clothier Road, Brislington, Bristol, BS4 5RL.

Worship

Groups may wish to spend more group time in worship and this is left to the discretion of the leader who will need to take this into account as the session is planned.

Keeping the group open

There is always a danger that a small group of people, developing a close relationship between its members, will become isolated from those outside, and this should be guarded against. It is hoped that groups will 'open their doors' to those around them – friends, neighbours, children of group members, relations. Special evenings can be arranged every so often – perhaps once every one or two months – when the programme focuses around a meal, coffee and chat or some of the all-age 'fun' activities published in the *Families* section of this leader's guide. You never know . . . others may want to join your study group as a result of these events!

Moving on

When your group has finished *Basics* and/or *I Believe* you might like to move on to the other books in this Serendipity series – details can be found on page 4; however, *these use a different method of study* and you may prefer to try a different series of Serendipity books. Contact Scripture Union for details. Whatever material you move on to think about the Group Covenant – does it need renewing for another period of time?

What's in a Session?

Each Bible study session in *Basics* and *I Believe* contains the following elements:

Introduction: this is material for the leader. In *Basics* it outlines the thinking behind the session, explaining how the session follows the diamond model, and suggests an 'icebreaker' to be used at the start of the session to help people relax and to encourage participation. The icebreakers are optional but they will help your group's study to be more effective.

Checklist for the leader: a guide to leading the session, divided into: preparation before the session, hints on what to do during the session, and follow-up after the session.

The Goal: in a sentence explains the point of the session.

Relational Bible Study: gently takes people into the Bible story and encourages group members to think about their own experiences and how they are different or similar to those of the biblical characters.

Deeper Bible Study: found only in *I Believe* and takes the group more deeply into the passage being studied.

Application: found in the later studies in *Basics* and *I Believe*; it encourages members to put their learning into practice.

Affirmation: a section that appears in some studies which encourages the group to affirm its members using the Bible teaching or some other exercise. For further explanation of this element of Bible study see Session 2 of the Training Course.

Timing: as leader you may use the study to fit the time available. Each session can be completed in an hour or may be used to fill an hour and a half. If you are serving coffee/a meal during the evening this will need extra time, as will any worship and prayer planned for the evening.

Training

6 SESSIONS TO TRAIN YOUR LEADERSHIP TEAM AND GROUP LEADERS

TRAINING

ORIENTATION: What is a Leadership Team for?

Objective: To get acquainted, introduce the concept of team ministry, take a "guided tour" of the entire programme, and agree on a contract for the next 5 training sessions.

Setting: Informal—minister's office or home, with moveable chairs—4 to 6 people per group

Time: About 90 minutes

☐ Group Building Game / 25-30 Minutes

☐ Content / 15-20 Minutes

☐ Group Discussion / 35-45 Minutes

Materials required: The Bible Study Course. *Serendipity Bible studies for small groups,* for everyone. Refreshments optional.

Leadership: The pastor or coordinator for ALL groups in the church should lead the training programme. This person must have experience in koinonia groups (Bible study + house groups) and be familiar with the Serendipity model for group-building in the first few weeks of a Bible study group. If possible, this person should attend one of the training workshops put on by Scripture Union Training Unit, 9-11 Clothier Road, Brislington, Bristol. BS4 5RL. Telephone: (0272) 719107.

End result: At the conclusion of this session, participants should be: (1) familiar with the programme, (2) familiar with the model for starting Bible study groups, and (3) open to the possibility of being on the Leadership Team.

Entertainment

FOR 1 POINT: I would be more likely to:
- a. go out to see a new film
- b. stay in and watch a T.V. re-run

FOR 2 POINTS: On T.V. I would choose:
- a. Coronation Street
- b. Evening News
- c. Wildlife on one

FOR 3 POINTS: If a film gets frightening I usually:
- a. close my eyes
- b. leave the room
- c. clutch a friend
- d. love it

FOR 4 POINTS: The films I prefer are:
- a. musicals
- b. comedies
- c. Walt Disney cartoons
- d. serious drama
- e. horror

FOR 5 POINTS: My idea of a good family time is:
- a. family picnic
- b. camping trip
- c. playing in the garden
- d. sitting round the fire

Ideals

FOR 1 POINT: If I had a choice I would:
- a. inherit a million pounds to spend
- b. make a million to give away

FOR 2 POINTS: I would choose a life of:
- a. happiness
- b. success
- c. riches
- d. adventure

FOR 3 POINTS: The person who most represents my ideals is:
- a. John Wayne
- b. Princess Diana
- c. Margaret Thatcher
- d. Alf Garnet
- e. John F. Kennedy

FOR 4 POINTS: If I chose a song title for my life it would be:
- a. All you need is love
- b. I am a rock, I am an island
- c. Make somebody happy
- d. If I had a hammer

FOR 5 POINTS: In my family I see myself as the:
- a. funny face
- b. wish bone (visionary)
- c. back bone
- d. neck bone (sticking my neck out)

Clothes

FOR 1 POINT: For clothes, I am more likely to go to:
- a. Marks and Spencer
- b. Moss Bros.

FOR 2 POINTS: I feel more comfortable wearing:
- a. formal clothes
- b. sports clothes
- c. casual clothes
- d. dirty jeans

FOR 3 POINTS: In buying clothes, I look first for:
- a. fashion / style
- b. name brand
- c. price
- d. quality

FOR 4 POINTS: If I buy the expensive "top of the line" in anything it is:
- a. socks
- b. underwear
- c. shoes
- d. suit/dress
- e. sportswear

FOR 5 POINTS: In buying clothes, I usually:
- a. shop all day for a bargain
- b. choose one store but try on everything
- c. buy the first thing I try on
- d. buy without trying it on

Taste

FOR 1 POINT: In music, I am closer to:
- a. Bach
- b. Beatles

FOR 2 POINTS: In furniture, I prefer:
- a. genuine antique
- b. reproduction
- c. Scandinavian—contemporary
- d. hotch potch—little of everything

FOR 3 POINTS: My choice of reading matter is:
- a. science fiction
- b. sports
- c. crime
- d. romance
- e. history

FOR 4 POINTS: If I had £1000 to splurge, I would buy:
- a. one original painting
- b. two prints
- c. three reproductions and an easy chair
- d. four cheap imitations, easy chair, and a colour T.V.

FOR 5 POINTS: In our family, we put a premium on:
- a. good education
- b. getting ahead
- c. quality time together
- d. simple life-style
- e. culture

Romance

FOR 1 POINT: I would prefer:
- a. blind date
- b. my second choice

FOR 2 POINTS: In dating, I prefer:
- a. going steady
- b. playing the field
- c. being close friends

FOR 3 POINTS: I prefer to marry someone who is:
- a. generous
- b. rich
- c. beautiful/handsome
- d. has a sense of humour
- e. intelligent

FOR 4 POINTS: I would choose for a honeymoon:
- a. South Sea Island
- b. walking in the Scottish Highlands
- c. camping in the Lakes
- d. Blackpool
- e. save money for a down-payment on a house

FOR 5 POINTS: My idea of a beautiful relationship is:
- a. Kermit and Miss Piggy
- b. Cinderella and Prince Charming
- c. The Waltons
- d. Don Quixote and Aldonza
- e. Andy Cap and Flo

Travel

FOR 1 POINT: When it comes to travel, I prefer:
- a. excitement
- b. enrichment

FOR 2 POINTS: On a holiday, my lifestyle is:
- a. go, go all the time
- b. party every night and sleep in
- c. slow and easy

FOR 3 POINTS: In packing for a trip, I include:
- a. toothbrush and change of underwear
- b. light bag and good book
- c. small suitcase and nice outfit
- d. all but the kitchen sink

FOR 4 POINTS: If I had £100 to blow, I would choose:
- a. one glorious night in a luxury hotel
- b. weekend in a nice hotel
- c. full week in a cheap hotel
- d. two weeks camping in the Lake District

FOR 5 POINTS: My idea of a great family holiday is:
- a. Butlins
- b. sailing on the Broads
- c. going to see the Grandparents
- d. skiing holiday
- e. staying home and having fun together

Habits

FOR 1 POINT: I am more likely to take a:
- a. shower
- b. bath

FOR 2 POINTS: I am more likely to squeeze the toothpaste:
- a. in the middle
- b. from the end
- c. roll it up

FOR 3 POINTS: If lost, I will probably:
- a. stop and ask directions
- b. check the map
- c. find the way by driving around

FOR 4 POINTS: I read the paper starting with:
- a. cartoons
- b. sports
- c. world news
- d. local news
- e. editorial
- f. entertainment guide
- g. crossword puzzle

FOR 5 POINTS: When I undress at night, I put my clothes:
- a. on a hanger in the wardrobe
- b. folded neatly over chair
- c. stuffed into laundry bag
- d. tossed in corner
- e. left on floor

Cars

FOR 1 POINT: My car is likely to be:
- a. spotless
- b. messy

FOR 2 POINTS: The part of my car that I keep in the best condition is:
- a. outside paint job
- b. interior
- c. engine

FOR 3 POINTS: I am more likely to buy a:
- a. luxury car—10 mpg
- b. sports car—20 mpg
- c. economy car—30 mpg
- d. tiny car—40 mpg

FOR 4 POINTS: If I had a choice of antique cars, I would choose:
- a. 1955 pink T-bird
- b. 1952 red MG-TD convertible
- c. 1937 silver Rolls Royce
- d. 1929 Model A Ford

FOR 5 POINTS: I think the best car for our family would be:
- a. Luv Bug
- b. Chitty Chitty Bang Bang
- c. turbo-charged Ferrari
- d. homemade camping caravan
- e. circus van

Work

FOR 1 POINT: I prefer to work at a job that is:
- a. too big to handle
- b. too small to challenge

FOR 2 POINTS: The job that is like work is:
- a. cleaning house
- b. working in the garden
- c. balancing my accounts

FOR 3 POINTS: In choosing a job, I look first for:
- a. salary
- b. security
- c. fulfilment
- d. working conditions

FOR 4 POINTS: If I had to choose between these jobs, I would choose:
- a. pickle inspector at processing plant
- b. complaint office at department store
- c. bedpan changer at hospital
- d. dustbin man
- e. personnel manager in charge of firing

FOR 5 POINTS: If my family could start a business, we would be good at:
- a. small general store
- b. family run restaurant
- c. day care centre
- d. circus troupe
- e. disco

Food

FOR 1 POINT: I prefer to eat in:
- a. Wimpy bar
- b. posh restaurant

FOR 2 POINTS: On the menu, I look for something:
- a. familiar
- b. different
- c. way out

FOR 3 POINTS: When eating chicken, I start with:
- a. leg
- b. breast
- c. gizzard
- d. liver

FOR 4 POINTS: I draw the line when it comes to eating:
- a. frogs legs
- b. pickled pigs feet
- c. sweet bread
- d. snails
- e. oysters
- f. raw herring

FOR 5 POINTS: When my family eats at home, I prefer:
- a. spaghetti
- b. meat and potatoes
- c. hamburgers
- d. salad
- e. casserole

1. If a large class, divide into smaller groups of from 4 to 6 each.

2. FIRST PERSON: Choose ONE category, such as Entertainment.

3. Read the 1 point question aloud to the group.

4. Everyone tries to GUESS your answer BEFORE you explain.

5. All who guessed RIGHT win 1 point each. Keep score of the points you win in the margin of your book.

6. Read the 2 points question and ask the group to guess. Those who guess right get 2 points.

7. Read through all questions in the category. Those who guess right on any question get the specified points.

8. NEXT PERSON: Choose another category.

9. Read the 1 point question. Before you explain, let others try to guess. Those who guess right win 1 point.

10. WINNER: When everyone in your group has read a category, add up the individual scores. The person with the most points wins.

HINT: *To make the game even more fun, divide your group into two teams and combine the individual scores within your team to determine the team winner.*

GROUP BUILDING GAME
Groups of 4 to 8 / 25-30 Minutes

Quiz

Rationale: Getting acquainted is twice the fun if you can do it in a guessing game. In Quiz, the others in your group try to guess what your answer will be BEFORE you explain.

CONTENT
All Together / 15-20 Minutes

What is a Leadership Team?

1. A Hand-Picked Group
The Leadership Team is a group of people or couples who have been personally recruited by the minister or church elder to oversee the ministry of small Bible study groups in the church.

The Leadership Team members are not the "spiritual giants" in the church, but they should be people who have demonstrated a genuine desire for their own spiritual growth and for the spiritual growth of the church through koinonia groups.

2. Committed to Spiritual Growth - Together
The Leadership Team's number 1 priority is your own life together as a spiritual growth group. Beginning with this programme for one year and continuing as an ongoing Bible study and support group, the group meets weekly (except for the summer) to share the Bible, pray, and support one another in your spiritual disciplines.

AT A GLANCE

MINISTER OR CO-ORDINATOR
A minister, elder, or co-ordinator with the backing of the church to co-ordinate the groups.

LEADERSHIP TEAM
A handful of people committed to the development of koinonia groups, beginning with their own spiritual growth as a group.

KOINONIA GROUPS
Groups of 6 to 8 people who agree to meet together once a week for Bible study and support in their spiritual growth, led by someone from the Leadership Team in the first few weeks.

EXTENDED FAMILY MONTHLY OUTREACH
Once a month, the Bible study group gets together for a potluck supper or outing with all of their spouses, children, and "extended family" — using one of the programmes on pages 73-95.

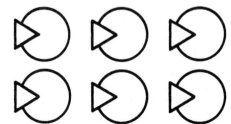
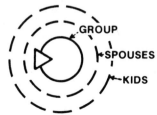

GROUP
SPOUSES
KIDS

3. Committed to Developing Bible Study Growth Groups

The next priority of the Leadership Team is to assist the minister in the cultivation of Bible study groups in the church. The Leadership Team is responsible not only for the promotion of Bible study groups, but also for the leadership of these groups in the first crucial weeks of formation.

In a sense, the Leadership Team is a group of group pediatricians. When new groups are formed (once or twice a year), the Leadership Team provides the group leaders for the first few weeks—until the groups are able to function on their own. Then, the group leader returns to the Leadership Team . . . or resigns from the Leadership Team and stays with the new group.

4. Long-range Development

The long-range dream of these Koinonia Groups (Bible study and house groups) is to expand into on-going extended families, with the spouses, children and other relatives, neighbours and friends, joining in monthly get togethers (see box opposite this page).

It will help if the minister, elders, church council, etc., are already in total agreement with this idea.

GROUP DISCUSSION
All Together / 30-45 Minutes

Guided Tour of This Course

Leader: Take the group on a page by page survey of this workbook, beginning with the overview of the course (pages 3 and 4). In the box on this page you will find the important pages highlighted. Spend 15 or 20 minutes in this "guided tour." Then, ask for questions.

Questions about the course's background and theology are answered on pages 5-7.

Remember, a person can come to the training programme for the Leadership Team without committing himself/herself to be on the Team. This commitment is called for after the sixth session.

Before this session is over, you should agree where and when you are going to hold the next training session and if you want to invite others to come.

GUIDED TOUR OF THIS COURSE:

At the first training session the leader should conduct a guided tour through the programme to give the Leadership Team the overall picture. Here are some of the highlights you need to look at.

Page 4: Here's the programme for a Bible study group at a glance.

• Beginner Units I and II: 6 weeks each. A group can take one or both. The purpose: to get acquainted and examine what you believe. No homework. The group is led by someone from the Leadership Team.

• Advanced Units III, IV, V, and VI: The group can continue for 40 more weeks. Homework required. The responsibility for leadership reverts to the group. The original leader can return to the Leadership Team or resign from the Leadership Team and stay with the group.

☐ Unit III: Epistle of Ephesians - 11 weeks

☐ Unit IV: Gospel of Mark - 17 weeks

☐ Unit V: Psalms - 6 weeks

☐ Unit VI: Old Testament - 6 weeks

Pages 5-7: Introducing the Serendipity method, and giving advice on how to organise and run a Serendipity group.

Page 41: Unit I/Basics: Purpose — to get acquainted. Six weeks. Covenant required — page 42. Study table of contents — page 43 and session one. Note that the agenda has two options and a box for the Leader.

Page 57: Unit II/I Believe: Purpose — to examine what you believe on the Apostles' Creed and share your own "faith journey." This unit can be substituted for Unit I for the first 6 weeks of a Beginner group.

Units III-VI are sold individually, available from Scripture Union Distribution.

Unit III/Epistles: Purpose — to study Ephesians and learn how to study any epistolary literature. Requires homework, shared leadership, and a monthly get-together with spouses and/or kids.

Unit IV/Gospels: Purpose — to study Mark and learn how to study short narrative material in the Bible. The study method is called chapter analysis.

Unit V/Psalms: Purpose — to study six selected psalms and learn how to study poetic material in the Bible. The Bible study method is called poetic stanza analysis.

Unit VI/Old Testament: Purpose — to study Genesis and learn how to study historical material in the Old Testament. The Bible study method is historical survey.

Training Programme: Explain the contents of the next 5 sessions:

• *Session 2:* Serendipity Groups: What's the big idea? - page 14.

• *Session 3:* Church Evaluation: Why do we need Bible study growth groups? - page 20.

• *Session 4:* Starting Right: How do we get started and keep going? - page 24.

• *Session 5:* Group Disciplines: Why do we need a group covenant? - page 30.

• *Session 6:* Leadership Team: Where do I fit in? - page 34.

Questions: Ask if there are any questions about the programme or the responsibility of the Leadership Team.

Close: Invite everyone to come to the training sessions for the next 5 weeks before deciding if God is calling them to be on the Leadership Team. Pass the books around and have everyone sign their name and phone number on page 40.

SERENDIPITY GROUPS: What's the big idea?

Objective: To understand the theory behind the Serendipity group-building model and to share the story of your spiritual journey with one another.

Setting: Small clusters around tables—4 to 6 people in each cluster—such as a group around dining table, another around kitchen table, etc.

Time: About 90 minutes
- ☐ Group Building Game / 25-30 Minutes
- ☐ Content / 15-20 Minutes
- ☐ Group Sharing / 30-35 Minutes
- ☐ Summing Up / 10-15 Minutes

Materials required:
- ☐ Book for everyone
- ☐ One dice or spinner for each group of 4-6 people
- ☐ One cup of crayons for each group

Leadership: The minister or coordinator of groups should lead this session. The content (groupwork diamond) is extremely important. The leader needs to understand the concept BEFORE trying to explain it.

End result: At the conclusion of this session, group members should (1) know each other's spiritual roots and early spiritual experience, (2) understand the "groupwork diamond" concept of group building, and (3) be on their way to "first stage" as a group.

ABOUT...

...YOUR GROWING UP...

...YOUR SPECIAL RELATIONSHIPS.

6...your best and worst subjects in school.

7...your favourite game when you were a kid.

8...your favourite pet or hobby.

9...the family holiday you remember most

10...the most shocking thing you ever did at a party

11...the time you got caught by your parents doing something really bad.

12...the sport you were best at.

13...your first job and how much you got.

14...the first time you tried to smoke.

15...the favourite meeting place when you were a teenager

16...the Christmas present you will always remember... and what was special about Christmas for you.

17...the person you could talk to about your problems when you were growing up.

18...your most embarrassing moment when you were a teenager.

19...the minister, S.S. teacher or youth leader who really influenced you.

20...your first dance...and what you wore.

21...the first time you were kissed outside the family.

22...the place where you went to do the things your parents disapproved of

CHURCH

GROUP BUILDING GAME
Groups of 4 to 6/25-30 Minutes

Tell Us About

Rationale: Possibly the best way to understand what we want out of a small caring group is to recall some of the significant relationships and groups in our past. This game is designed to let you talk about these beautiful memories.

Instructions:

1. Get a counter (a penny, key, etc.) and put it on START.

2. Roll the dice or spinner and advance your mover. Stop and explain or answer the half-finished sentence you land on.

3. To reach the Finish Line, you must roll the exact number that puts you on the Finish Line.

CONTENT
All Together/15-20 Minutes

Theory Behind the Serendipity Group Model

A Serendipity Group is a small caring community of 6 to 8 people who are willing to get serious about their spiritual growth. Like a weight watcher's group, the members "covenant" together to keep a set of spiritual disciplines for a specific number of weeks. The disciplines include Bible study and a weekly meeting to report to the group on each one's spiritual progress.

This course provides a rigorous programme of individual and group disciplines for a year. In the last session we walked through this course—unit by unit—and saw the development of the Bible study methodology. In this session, we want to look at the first unit—Basics—and study the rationale behind the first six weeks of the "group building" process.

No Mystery

A Christian community where there is *real* love, *real* caring, *real* sharing, *real* healing—this is what we all yearn for, but seldom experience.

When we do experience this spiritual oneness, we don't understand why. We often say, "the Holy Spirit brought us together," but we assume the reason *why* and *how* is beyond comprehension. This is unfortunate, because there are basic principles involved in "becoming" a Christian community, and it can happen anytime, anywhere—whenever these principles are followed.

Like a Baseball or Rounders Diamond

To understand what is involved, picture in your mind a rounders pitch or a baseball diamond. At the home base write the word "Koinonia." This is the Greek word for perfect oneness in Christ. It refers to a marriage-like relationship in Christ in which there is total openness and freedom to be yourself; to share joy and pain without fear of being judged or ridiculed or laughed at; and to experience what the "body of Christ" is all about—deep spiritual community. This is the aim of Serendipity groups. This is the essence of the groupwork diamond.

First Stage/Story Telling

To get to Koinonia, you have to go around each corner of the diamond, which is another way of saying that there is a process to becoming a group. First stage in this process might be called "Story Telling."

This phase is so basic that it is often forgotten until group members wake up months later and wonder why they feel like strangers to one another. In a few words, history giving is "telling your story" to one another.

☐ *Your past:* where you have come from—your roots, heritage, significant people, places, and events that contributed to the person you are today.

☐ *Your present:* where you are right now in your spiritual journey—your interests, values, concerns, and struggles.

☐ *Your future:* where you are headed—the things you long for, work for, and pray for.

If you look closely at the lesson plans for the first three sessions in Unit I, you will see how we have programmed the sharing for historygiving. The two optional "conversation starters" and the Bible study are designed to help group members tell their "story." Even in the Bible study, the emphasis is upon how this "story" in Scripture reminds you of your "story."

In the process of telling your "story" to the group, the group not only gets to know you, but also gets to *feel* a part of your life . . . and you get to *feel* a part of their lives. A oneness and closeness develops. You realize that you are not alone. Your story, though unfinished, is accepted. You are accepted. You are on your way as a group.

Second Stage/Affirmation

After three weeks at the first stage, the group is ready to move on to the second stage. We call the second stage "Affirmation," which is another word for saying *positive* feedback. Here, the group is given the opportunity to respond to each other's "story."

☐ *Appreciation:* "what I appreciate about you and your story"

☐ *Strengths:* "what I see as the strong points in your life and story"

☐ *Feelings:* "what I feel about you and your story"

Sharing *positive* feelings for one another should be a part of any relationship (especially in a small, caring group). This is doubly important in a group-building situation where everyone has shared the significant pages of his/her "story"—some of it painful or "never shared before."

Thus, in the fourth session, we reverse the process and have an entire session built around affirmation. (See pages 50-51, "Happiness Is," especially the instructions for AFFIRMATION and HOW TO SHARE at the bottom of page 51.)

Jesus constantly used affirmation in his ministry, especially with people who were "down on themselves" or felt worthless. Look at the story of:

☐ *Simon* in John 1:40-42. Jesus saw in him a "rock" and changed his name to Peter when Simon thought of himself as a "sinful man" (Luke 5:8).

- *Nathanael* in John 1:47-51. Jesus said of this lowly "nobody," ". . . Here is a true Israelite, in whom there is nothing false." Wow!

- *Zacchaeus* in Luke 19:1-10. Jesus called this "little man" (up a tree) a "son of Abraham" . . . somebody I would like to get to know better over dinner. Look how his behavior changed after that dinner.

- *The prostitute* in Luke 7:36-47. The Pharisee saw this girl as "unclean," but Jesus saw in her a beautiful person . . . BECAUSE HE SAW WHAT THE GIRL WAS "BECOMING" (which is the real meaning of prophecy).

As the group moves deeper into sharing your "stories" at third base, the principle of affirmation will be more and more significant. In fact, the principle of affirmation underlies the whole of the sharing process as the group learns to do for each other what Jesus Christ is doing in our lives.

Hearing from the members of a group that you are "beautiful . . . appreciated . . . worthwhile . . . and a person of great potential" will enable you to say, "Yes . . . I am worthwhile . . . I have unique gifts . . . I can, I will be what I am called to be in Christ."

Third Stage/Goal Setting

The third stage in the group-building process is "Goal Setting." This is another way of saying "need sharing."

- Where are you struggling in your spiritual life?

- Where do you need to grow?

- Where do you need to be healed?

- What is God telling you to do?

If you asked these kinds of questions at the beginning of the group, you would scare everyone to death. You just don't talk about your needs to strangers. However, when you have established a trust and confidence in one another, it is only natural to share these things. In fact, if you withhold this information from the group, you have nullified the very purpose of the group—to support one another in your spiritual struggles.

So, in the fifth session (see page 52-53, "Asking and Receiving"), the opportunity is given for you to share with the group the area in your life that needs some work. The optional conversation starters start the process, and the Bible study exercise allows you to walk through a Bible "story" into your own "story."

The Introduction on page 50 explains more

about the ministry of the group at this point, based on the "plus" that is provided through the Holy Spirit to minister to one another. The Holy Spirit has endowed every Christian with a "spiritual gift" for ministry in the "body of Christ." Some people are especially gifted in "prophecy." Others in "service . . . teaching . . . exhorting . . . giving . . . administering . . . and empathizing." (See session 6, page 54.)

Once a person shares a goal or need, it is up to the group to support this person in this goal. This is the basis for the spiritual discipline of "accountability" in the covenant that every group member signs. (See page 42.) Accountability means that you give permission to the group to hold you accountable to do what you said you would do.

Goal setting and accountability are what make a Serendipity group life-changing. When you start to get serious about your spiritual growth and are willing to commit yourself each week to deeper and deeper goals before God and the members of the group, and the group starts to take their responsibility seriously, a whole new ball game emerges. And the winner will be you.

Koinonia

This brings the group to "Koinonia." Oneness. Spiritual union and communion — with Christ and with one another. This is the music of Pentecost that was heard when the broken followers of Christ got together in an "upper room" to bind up the wounds of one another, share their pain, shattered dreams, and feelings of failure. Not for *one* day like we celebrate in the church. But for 50 days — until something "happened."

This does not mean that the group will never experience conflict, any more than a happy marriage is without conflict. But there will be a new basis on which you will be able to deal with conflict: (1) understanding each other's story — the reason why you are who you are, (2) affirming each other's strengths, and (3) supporting each other in the goals you have set for yourselves.

This is what a Serendipity group is all about. That is what this programme is all about. Becoming a caring community. Agreeing on a common spiritual discipline. Telling your "story" to each other. Supporting each other in your struggles. Rejoicing in your good times. Reaching out to each other in your bad times. Being to one another the ministers of Jesus Christ.

Leader: Encourage questions and discussion about the groupwork diamond concept of group building. Make sure everyone understands how a group goes through the stages in the first unit.

GROUP SHARING
Groups of 3 or 4/30 to 40 Minutes

My Spiritual Story

Leader: Before the session draw your own spiritual pilgrimage, using the instructions below. When the time comes for this exercise, "show and tell" your spiritual pilgrimage to the whole group. Go into great detail about your early spiritual beginnings. The "turning points" in your spiritual formation. And where you are right now. Set the pace for real openness and honesty by your model. Then, pass out the crayons and ask everyone to draw their spiritual pilgrimage IN SILENCE.

Instructions:

1. Think over the spiritual ups and downs in your life—from as far back as you can recall to the present—and try to tell the story of your spiritual life in a drawing on the next page.

2. Begin with the place where your first memories of God start. Draw a house, a church, or a symbol of this time in your life such as a flower. *Colour* in the figure to represent the *feelings*—such as light green to represent early growth, or a bright orange to represent warm feelings.

3. Move to the next period in your spiritual pilgrimage. Think of a symbol or colour to represent this period (such as a big question mark—coloured in with grey).
   Try to portray every period in your spiritual life—and the TURNING POINTS—with a different *symbol* and *colour*. Remember, colour is FEELING.

4. You will have 10 minutes IN SILENCE to draw your spiritual pilgrimage. Then, you will have an opportunity to "show and tell" your spiritual story.

Leader: After 10 minutes, call time and explain the rest of these instructions.

5. Split into groups of 3 or 4. Rearrange your chairs—close together.

6. Turn your book around so that the others are looking directly at your drawing.

7. Start with the early beginnings. Explain your choice of symbol and colour. Then, go to the

17

SAMPLES

To draw your spiritual pilgrimage, you can choose from a number of art forms. Here are a few.

STICK FIGURES: Show the ups and downs in your spiritual life by drawing little stick figures in various positions and expressions.

ROAD MAP: Show your journey like a road map with the early beginnings, the mountain tops, the dark valleys, the fork in the road, and the place where you are right now. Then add symbols to tell the story.

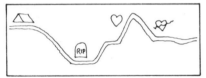

GRAPH LINE: This is probably the easiest way to tell your spiritual pilgrimage—with a line that goes up and down like a profit and loss statement.

SYMBOLS: Divide your spiritual life into three or four periods and describe each one with a symbol, such as a rainbow for happiness, a cloud for rainy days, a streak of lightning for crisis, and a question mark for doubt.

REMEMBER, USE COLOURS TO DESCRIBE THE FEELINGS FOR EACH PERIOD IN YOUR SPIRITUAL LIFE. COLOUR IS FEELING.

18

next period in your spiritual story, etc., until you have explained your drawing in detail.

8. When the first person in your group has finished, stop and let the others respond by finishing this sentence:

   "The gift that you gave to me in your story was...."

   For example: "The gift that you gave to me in your story was the part about growing up in an old fashioned Christian home where you read the Bible at the supper table." Or, "The gift that you gave to me was sharing some of your pain right now...."

   (In responding this way, you are really AFFIRMING the person who has shared their story by responding with your *positive feelings* for the person.)

9. Then, move to the next person. Let this person share his/her story. Then, let the group respond to this person, etc.

10. Leader: Tell the group they have approximately _____ minutes (fill in the time) and this means everyone in your group will have _____ minutes. Move in close and proceed. [Allow at least 10 minutes per person for sharing.]

SUMMING UP
All Together / 10 Minutes

What I Learned

Leader: Get everyone together at the close for feedback. Go around and let everyone finish one of these two sentences:

   ☐ *In this session, I learned....*

   ☐ *In this session, I discovered....*

Take care of any unfinished business and close in prayer.

MY SPIRITUAL STORY: Described in a drawing . . . showing my spiritual ups and downs.

TRAINING

CHURCH EVALUATION:
Why do we need Bible study growth groups?

Objective: To evaluate the needs of people in your community and your church; to evaluate what your church is doing right now to meet these needs; to brainstorm ways of providing small, caring communities for everyone in your church.

Setting: Groups of 6 or 8, around tables or in small clusters.

Time: About 90 minutes
- ☐ Group Building Game/25 - 30 Minutes
- ☐ Content/15 - 20 Minutes
- ☐ Group Sharing/25 - 30 Minutes
- ☐ Summing up/10-15 Minutes

Materials required
- ☐ Book for everyone
- ☐ Pencils

Leadership: The leader for this session must be prepared to present the Content material, asking the people to underline important points as they follow along in their book. Personal examples or discussion questions could be added by the leader.

End result: At the conclusion of this session the Leadership Team should: (1) know where people in the community are hurting, (2) know where the people in the church are hurting, (3) know where people in your own Leadership Team are hurting, and (4) be on the way toward thinking through a strategy for a network of small, caring communities in your church.

OUR COMMUNITY

As soon as the question is read, respond with the first thing that pops into your mind. Let the answers in your group go off like fire crackers.

WHAT DO THE PEOPLE IN OUR COMMUNITY...
1. want out of life?
2. talk about over coffee?
3. get excited about?
4. worry about?
5. hold in high esteem?
6. expect out of the church?
7. yearn for?
8. do with their problems?

WHERE DO THE PEOPLE IN OUR COMMUNITY...
1. gather for coffee?
2. get their values?
3. go for escape?
4. go when they are lonely?
5. go when they are hurting?
6. go for deep, meaningful relationships?
7. look for meaning and purpose in life?
8. call when their world caves in on them?

WHO DO THE PEOPLE IN OUR COMMUNITY...
1. listen to for advice and counsel?
2. blame for their problems?
3. look up to as a real model of success?
4. talk to about their family problems?
5. confide in about their deepest longings?
6. call upon at 3 o'clock in the morning for help?
7. go to for spiritual direction?
8. turn to for unconditional love and acceptance?

WHY DO THE PEOPLE IN OUR COMMUNITY...
1. spend so much on adult toys?
2. get hooked on alcohol and drugs?
3. live over their heads financially?
4. drop out of church?
5. get sexually involved?
6. go to the pub with their problems?
7. find life so boring?
8. avoid deep spiritual commitment?

OUR CHURCH

As soon as the question is read, respond with the first thing that pops into your mind. Let the answers in your group go off like fire crackers.

WHAT DO THE PEOPLE IN OUR CHURCH...

1. want out of life?
2. talk about over coffee?
3. get excited about?
4. worry about?
5. hold in high esteem?
6. expect out of our church?
7. yearn for?
8. do with their problems?

WHERE DO THE PEOPLE IN OUR CHURCH...

1. gather for coffee?
2. get their values?
3. go for escape?
4. go when they are lonely?
5. go when they are hurting?
6. go for deep, meaningful relationships?
7. look for meaning and purpose in life?
8. call when their world caves in on them?

WHO DO THE PEOPLE IN OUR CHURCH...

1. listen to for advice and counsel?
2. blame for their problems?
3. look up to as a real model of success?
4. talk to about their family problems?
5. confide in about their deepest longings?
6. call upon at 3 o'clock in the morning for help?
7. go to for spiritual direction?
8. turn to for unconditional love and acceptance?

WHY DO THE PEOPLE IN OUR CHURCH...

1. spend so much on adult toys?
2. get hooked on alcohol and drugs?
3. live over their head financially?
4. drop out of church?
5. get sexually involved?
6. go to a non-Christian friend with their problems?
7. find life boring?
8. avoid deep spiritual commitment?

OUR GROUP

as soon as the question is read, respond with the first thing that pops into your mind. Let the answers in your group go off like fire crackers.

WHAT DO THE PEOPLE IN OUR GROUP (RIGHT HERE)...

1. want out of life?
2. talk about over coffee?
3. get excited about?
4. worry about?
5. hold in high esteem?
6. expect out of the church?
7. yearn for?
8. do with our problems?

WHERE DO THE PEOPLE IN OUR GROUP...

1. gather for coffee?
2. get our values?
3. go for escape?
4. go when we are lonely?
5. go when we are hurting?
6. go for deep, meaningful relationships?
7. look for meaning and purpose in life?
8. call when our world caves in on us?

WHO DO THE PEOPLE IN OUR GROUP...

1. listen to for advice and counsel?
2. blame for our problems?
3. look up to as a real model of success?
4. talk to about our family problems?
5. confide in about our deepest longings?
6. call upon at 3 o'clock in the morning for help?
7. go to for spiritual direction?
8. turn to for unconditional love and acceptance?

WHY DO THE PEOPLE IN OUR GROUP...

1. spend so much on adult toys?
2. get hooked on alcohol and drugs?
3. live over our heads financially?
4. drop out of church?
5. get sexually involved?
6. go to a non-Christian friend with our problems?
7. find life boring?
8. avoid deep spiritual commitment?

GROUP BUILDING GAME
Groups of 6 to 8/25-30 Minutes

Popcorn

Rationale: The strategy for Koinonia groups in your church should grow out of an understanding of what the people discern as their own immediate needs—which this firecracker quiz will bring out.

Instructions:

1. Gather in groups of 6 to 8.

2. Appoint one person in each group to act as the reader.

3. Reader: Start with the first column—Our Community—and read the first question. Ask everyone to respond with the first thing that pops into their head. The answers should go off like popcorn or firecrackers the instant the question is read. **Don't stop to analyse the answers.**

4. Repeat the process for the questions in ALL three columns.

CONTENT
All Together/15 Minutes

What's the Problem?

In session two we looked at the meaning of real community—koinonia. But even a casual observer will tell us that there is a large gap between real community and what we experience in the church. Let's take a look at some of the sociological factors that we have to live with today.

The Breakdown of the Family
The large extended family of two generations ago has been replaced by the nuclear family (father, mother and 2.2 children). Even with the nuclear family, nearly 50 percent of the people are living in single parent relationships. There is no sign that this percentage will decrease in the immediate future. Added to the divorce rate and the facts that people are waiting longer to get married and living longer after the death of a spouse, puts us in a country where over 50 percent of all adults are single.

The Breakdown of the Neighbourhood
The British ambition of a house in the right (nice) neighbourhood with the right neighbours and the right job has destroyed the traditional nature of the neighbourhood. With the average British family moving every five to eight years, there is no time to get to know the neighbours. Or just when relationships between neighbours are established, one or the other moves on.

The neighbourhood has fallen victims of the economic and social climate becoming a mini ghetto for certain economic, age, race, class, etc., groups. There is still a strong compulsion to "keep up with the Jones." So "loving my neighbour" is replaced with "keeping up with my neighbour."

The Overload on the Church
When your parents live a hundred miles away and your next-door neighbour is transferred every year, a lot of people are turning in desperation to their church to provide the emotional support for their survival system. The ministerial workers are often overwhelmed at the need: "There are just too many demands . . . and too few resources."

And in the midst of the overloaded circuits, it is virtually impossible to provide for all of the spiritual needs of the people with one kind of programme. People with special needs or deeper spiritual hunger are sometimes overlooked in the "conveyer belt" system of ministry in the church.

This is the reason why more and more churches are turning to small caring groups for spiritual growth and support.

Defining the Need
In thinking of a new style of caring communities, we need to redefine the need.

☐ *The need to know God:* Augustine said, "Man was made for fellowship with God, and he will be restless until he finds his rest in God." This is basic. Sometimes the church is too timid about the gospel. Without apology we need to sharpen our message: "Our purpose is to know God, and to make Jesus Christ, his Son, the Lord of our lives."

☐ *The need to be accepted:* Jesus Christ upset the religious crowd of his day by accepting a lot of unreligious people—the social outcasts, moral failures, alcoholics, drug pushers, prostitutes, and divorcees.

Unfortunately the church has given the impression that the membership is open only to "good" people. Somehow we have got to learn to say, "Neither do I condemn you . . . . Go, sin no more."

☐ *The need to be transformed:* Paul's agonizing cry is the cry of every person: "Oh wretched man that I am, who will deliver me from this law (rule) of sin." Romans 7:24. We don't have to be told that we have made a mess of our lives. We already know this. What we need to know is that we don't have to continue this way.

☐ *The need to belong.* Closely associated with the first three is this drive. Peer group pressure is not limited to the teen years. It dominates our lives. Anyone that says he can get along without a few friends is kidding himself.

The Early Church vs the Church Today
There are a great many parallels between the first century and the twentieth century. The church in the first century flourished. Why? Acts 2:42-47 may offer a clue. The early church was built around five basics:

1. *Bible study and prayer:* "They devoted themselves to the apostles' teaching and to fellowship, to the breaking of bread and prayer."

2. *Healing:* "Everyone was filled with awe, and many wonders and miraculous signs were done . . ."

3. *Concern for one another:* "All the believers were together and had everything in common. Selling their possessions and goods, they gave to everyone as he had need."

4. *Extended family:* "Every day they continued to meet together in the temple courts. They broke bread in their homes and ate together with glad and sincere hearts, praising God and enjoying the favour of all the people."

5. *Open family:* "And the Lord added to their number daily those who were being saved."

The Bob Paisley Magic
Bob Paisley brought a special magic to the football team he managed—Liverpool. He had the respect and confidence of the players, and he was a driving force. Many attribute Liverpool's success to his stimulus and direction. Where would Liverpool be now without Paisley? Would they be riding high or be a directionless second rate team? Some would see local churches today as organisations lacking Bob Paisleys—not knowing where they are going or what they want—directionless and grounded.

GROUP SHARING
Groups of 6 to 8/25-30 Minutes

Evaluation Questionnaire

Leader: Divide the group into the same small groups that played the game at the beginning of the session. Ask everyone to fill out the questionnaire in silence. Then, spend the rest of

the time (30 minutes) discussing the questionnaire, point by point.

SUMMING UP
All Together /10-15 Minutes

Brainstorming

Leader: Gather everyone at the close to brainstorm on the question:

☐ *What can we do to build a network of small Bible study and growth groups in our church?*

Remember, in brainstorming you do not stop to evaluate a suggestion. Don't let anybody pour "cold water" on an idea. Just keep brainstorming with better ideas.

At the close, deal with any business and close in prayer.

CHURCH ASSESSMENT QUESTIONNAIRE

CAR STICKERS: Choose two car stickers that convey the message of your church: (1) a car sticker for people in your community to see, (2) a car sticker for your own people to see.

_____ Honk if you love Jesus.
_____ To err is human . . . to forgive is out of the question.
_____ If you're looking for a friend, I'd like to apply.
_____ God loves you and I'm trying.
_____ Please have patience; God is not finished with me yet.
_____ I have abandoned my search for truth and am now looking for a good fantasy.
_____ We've found it.
_____ Wise men still seek him.
_____ Don't bug me. I'm pedaling as fast as I can.
_____ We must hurry and catch up, for we are the leaders.
_____ Have you hugged your children today?

COMPARISONS: Below are a series of allegories. Circle the one in each line that is more like your church.

My church is more like a. . . .
fancy restaurant . . . . home cooking
battlefield hospital . . . . fitness center
day care nursery . . . . army camp
one-man band . . . . Symphony Orchestra
down and outs drop-in centre . . . . exclusive businessmen's club

THE BOTTOM LINE: How would you evaluate your church ministry in these two areas? Put a dot on the line—somewhere in between the two extremes—to indicate how you see your church.

On leading people into a personal relationship with Jesus Christ.
Super weak _____ Super strong

On providing a deep, caring community where people can grow in their faith.
Super weak _____ Super strong

STRENGTHS: Rank the top three human assets in your church—1, 2, and 3.

_____ clear direction   _____ solid financial base
_____ strong leadership   _____ strong Bible study groups
_____ concern for outreach   _____ openness to new ideas
_____ good biblical foundation _____ commitment to the future
_____ dedicated workers

REACTIONS: Indicate how you feel about the statements below by circling a number from 1 to 10—1 being "I strongly agree" and 10 being "I strongly disagree."

Our church has a clear direction and most of the people know what it is.

1   2   3   4   5   6   7   8   9   10

Our church is committed to provide a support system for every person in which a person can belong, be accepted, and mature in the Christian faith.

1   2   3   4   5   6   7   8   9   10

THE BIBLE STUDY/CARING GROUP CONCEPT: How do you feel about the idea of providing small Bible study groups for anyone in the church who is serious about spiritual growth? (circle one)

a. great idea   d. we're not ready for this
b. O.K., but. . . .   e. ask me tomorrow
c. sounds like a lot of work

GOAL SETTING: What would a good coach do if he was in your situation? Jot down two things a coach would do to get things moving in your church in the direction of small caring communities.

Now, take one of these ideas from your coach and jot down two steps that could make this dream come true.

STARTING RIGHT: How do we get started and keep going?

Objective: To have fun affirming each other through a game; to learn how to start groups in your church; and to find out what is involved in the Leadership Team.

Setting: Small clusters of chairs—6 to 8 each—of people that know each other.

Time: About 90 minutes

- ☐ Group Affirmation Game / 25-30 Minutes
- ☐ Content / 15-20 Minutes
- ☐ Group Sharing / 25-30 Minutes
- ☐ Summing Up / 10-15 Minutes

Materials required:

- ☐ Book and pencil for everyone
- ☐ Small slip of paper for everyone
- ☐ Small bowl for each group of 6 to 8

Leadership: The coordinator for groups in the church should lead this session. This person should be familiar with the policy of the elders/ church council for initiating Koinonia groups, plus the church calendar for the autumn, winter, and spring programmes.

End result: At the conclusion of this session the group should know: (1) how to start small Koinonia groups, (2) what is involved in the Leadership Team, and (3) have a tentative plan for initiating groups in the church.

GROUP BUILDING GAME
Groups of 6 to 8 / 25-30 Minutes

Guess Who?

Rationale: After three sessions together you should know enough about each other to "affirm" each other (just as you would in the fourth session in a Beginner group). "Guess Who" is an affirmation game where a participant draws the name of another person and describes this person in terms of an animal, car, etc. Other

PLAYFUL PORPOISE
agile, intelligent, lively — the life of the party.

HONEY BEE
energetic, quick and tireless worker — nectar gatherer and pollen spreader.

PUPPY
soft, furry, fun loving, playful, irresistible—disarmingly childlike.

TIRELESS TURTLE
slow and steady, persistent plodder — willing to stick out his/her neck.

CUDDLY TEDDY BEAR
lovable, warm, playful — that brings out the "mother" in all of us.

INNOCENT LITTLE LAMB
dressed in the skin of a roaring lion with a big rough exterior to cover up a gentle, beautiful person inside.

1972 DUNE BUGGY
with sky blue sparkle paint and balloon tires, roll bar and bucket seats.

SURREY WITH THE FRINGE ON TOP
with embroidery, tassles, peek-a-boo curtains, the smell of jasmine and all things nice.

1960 FORD PREFECT
well cared for, reliable, with radio tuned to 60's music.

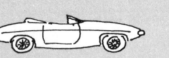

"E" TYPE
horse power enough to move a castle; streamlined, low, comfy seats, etc.

AMERICAN CHEVROLET
spacious, fast, with plush upholstery and every possible accessory.

1929 MODEL T FORD
with rumble seat and genuine leather upholstery, built to last and just as fun as the day it came from the factory.

TENACIOUS TUG BOAT
conscientious, unpretentious, workhorse of the docks — capable of pulling heavy loads and guiding big ships.

TOY SAIL BOAT
with paper sail — original, handmade, creative, childlike, authentic.

HIGHSPEED MOTORBOAT
awesome power but low profile — versatile and fun.

WOOD RAFT
unsinkable, homemade, unpretentious—yet built for lots of adventure.

CRUISING YACHT
sleek, posh, totally equipped for luxurious travel and deep sea sport.

VENETIAN GONDOLA
with love seat in the back and a moustached oarsman to guide through the romantic canals.

MOTHER HEN
warm, sensitive, sprightly, protective — always on the lookout for the well-being of others.

PEACEFUL, GENTLE DOVE
serene, calm in the midst of heavy storms.

WISE OLD OWL
quiet, thoughtful — with the appearance of being in deep contemplation.

FRIENDLY ROBIN
cheerful, perky, inquisitive, good humoured — with a nesting instinct.

LORDLY PEACOCK
colourful, spectacular — with a rainbow of plumage.

GRACEFUL SWAN
majestic, smooth-sailing, unruffled — always in command.

WILD EAGLE
untamed, noble — cherishes freedom and jealously guards independence.

HUNGRY CHEETAH
quiet, unassuming, sleek, on the prowl — usually gets his/her prey.

FAITHFUL SHEEP DOG
loyal, dependable, devoted — an abiding companion.

1941 RED MG
with bucket headlights and top open to the fresh air, tree green seat covers and a smell of spring.

1975 HARLEY DAVIDSON MOTORCYCLE
double seats, angled bars for laid-back driving, accelerates quickly from stop.

WELLS FARGO STAGECOACH

HOMEMADE CAMPING CARAVAN
with eye-catching ornaments hanging from the sides, and music and stories from a thousand romantic lands.

CUSTOM BUILT VAN
with floor to ceiling carpet, CB radio, stereo player, bunk beds, and floral wallpapering.

VOLKSWAGEN WITH ROLLS ROYCE FRONT
with retread tyres and white walls painted on, slightly incongruous and mischievous.

PORSCHE TURBO CARRARO
with air foils, spoilers and racing slicks, tuned to perfection and ready for the Le Mans.

SUGAR PLUM FAIRY MAKEBELIEVE CARRIAGE
with silvery wheels and diamond-studded trim, and a luggage rack of exotic magical items from far away lands.

CIRCUS CLOWN'S CAR
with horn blaring, fireworks exploding, fun songs issuing from the boot.

ARISTOCRATIC QUEEN ELIZABETH II
dignified, well-endowed luxury — extravagantly equipped but tasteful

MYTHICAL TREASURE SHIP
carrying hidden treasure and exotic spices, full of mystery and surprises and a little mischievous rum.

MISSISSIPPI RIVER FERRY BOAT
elegant, perfectly appointed, with minstrel music and the smell of perfume — quietly plying the waters.

OLD FASHIONED ROWING BOAT
uncomplicated, but sturdy — made for fishing in quiet ponds.

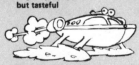

SLEEK HYDROFOIL
with jet engine for superfast gliding above rough waters or smooth sailing in calm waters.

AIRCRAFT CARRIER
sophisticated, awe inspiring, complex — equipped with the latest in technological advances.

RUBBER DINGHY
with makeshift paddle, compact, transportable, inflatable — fun to be in.

CLIPPER
even-keeled smooth-sailing, majestic queen — sails unfurled to catch the wind, gliding through deep waters with effortless composure.

members in the group then try to guess who was described. It's affirming and it's lots of fun.

Instructions:

1. Have everyone write their name on a slip of paper. Fold the slip of paper once and place it in a small bowl in the center of the group.

2. Stir up the slips of paper. Reach in and draw one slip of paper. DO NOT LET ANYONE KNOW THE NAME YOU HAVE PICKED.

3. For the person you have chosen, think of an ANIMAL that best describes this person. (If you wish, look over the ANIMALS on the game board—top section.)

ROUND ONE:

4. First person: Describe the person you have picked as an AMIMAL and let the others guess who this person is. Simply finish the sentence: "The person I have chosen is like a...."

5. Next person: Explain the person you have picked as an ANIMAL and let the others guess.

6. Continue around your group until everyone has explained the person they have as an ANIMAL.

ROUND TWO:

7. Put all slips of paper back into the bowl in the center of the group. Stir and pick a new slip of paper.

8. Go around and explain the person you picked as a CAR. Finish the sentence: "The person I have picked reminds me of a...." (You can use the sample CARS on the game board or make up a CAR to perfectly fit this person.) Then, the others in the group try to guess the person.

ROUND THREE:

9. Put all slips of paper back into the bowl. Stir and pick a new name.

10. Go around and explain the person you picked as a BOAT. Finish the sentence, "The person I have picked reminds me of a...." (You can choose one of the sample BOATS on the game board or make up a BOAT to perfectly describe this person.) Then, the others in the group try to guess the person.

CONTENT
All Together /15-20 Minutes

Ten Steps for Starting Groups

Sometimes a road map is essential. This is a road map to help you start small Koinonia groups in your church.

1. Decide on your objective. If you were planning a trip, the overall objective might be to get to a certain spot, such as the Colorado rockies. Or, to have fun, to take a rest, to spend some time with the family, or to explore a part of the world that you have not seen before.

In business, the objective might be to make money, or to expand your responsibility, or to make a contribution to your field of work.

Your objective must be specific, somewhat tangible and measurable. For example: your objective might be to provide an opportunity for everyone in your church to belong to a small caring Koinonia group. This decision needs to be made in consultation with the minister and elders/council or it will get nowhere. NOWHERE.

2. Break down the long-range objective into short-range goals. If your long-range objective is to drive from London to Dundee, your short-range goal might be to get to Leeds for lunch, Newcastle for tea time, Edinburgh for supper, and to arrive in Dundee before midnight. You now have a timetable to check that you are on schedule or not.

In the same way, if your long-range objective is to offer small Koinonia groups in your church, what are the short-range goals you want to set: (1) for the first 6 months, (2) for the next 6 months, etc.

3. Build a leadership team. This step should come first, but we are putting it here because you are probably at this step in the process already. You have probably been recruited especially to be on this leadership team, and this is the reason why you are in training right now.

In making this statement we are assuming that: (a) you have been recruited especially for this training, (b) your church is committed to the need for creating Koinonia groups in your church, and (c) you are open to the possibility of serving as a leader or "shepherd" to one of these Koinonia groups in the near future.

The Leadership Team's first priority is your own spiritual growth and support. The Leadership Team should meet weekly for Bible study—going through the programme for a year. Then, continue on your own in Bible study of your choice.

The second priority—to serve as leaders for Beginner groups in their first 6 or 12 weeks of existence. (After this time, the group switches to their own internal leadership.)

The third priority—to oversee and evaluate the health and balance of all the groups in your church, in connection with the minister and elders/council.

4. Decide how you are going to start. There are two basic ways to start groups in your church. Both have good points.

☐ The "amoeba" approach: Here, you start with one or two groups and let them multiply ... and multiply ... and multiply until you have a lot of groups. For instance, you might start with a men's group and a couple's group.

In the first few weeks each group is encouraged to draw in enough new people to split into four groups when they are ready to move into the Advanced units (the real part of the course—at Unit III).

This approach is easier, takes very little promotion and multiplies on the strength of its own enthusiasm. The people in the groups are their own best advertisement.

The drawback is the slow process. It may be three or four years before the groups are reaching very many people.

☐ The "big bang" approach: Here, you invite everyone in the church who wants to be in a Koinonia group to "sign up" for a Beginner group. All groups start on the same week. Then, any group that wishes to continue on in the Advanced units can do so if they sign the advanced Covenant.

The advantage of this approach is that you can start with as many groups as you have leaders.

The disadvantage is that you may get people into the groups in the crash programme that are really not ready for the deeper commitment. On the other hand, you may reach people in the crash programme that you would not reach for years in the other approach.

5. Assign leaders from the Leadership Team to the Beginner groups. The first few weeks of a group is crucial, just like the first few weeks of a child's life. Someone from the Leadership Team (who has already been through the first unit) needs to be on hand to lead the sessions.

The leadership is more like a pacesetter. The leader simply goes first in each sharing exercise. The first unit is spent in group building and the second unit is spent in examining your faith. The leader is there to see that the group stays to the agenda for each session.

Then, after the "trial" period, the group decides if they wish to continue. If they decide to continue, they start rotating the leadership around the group . . . and the original leader drops out, or resigns from the Leadership Team and remains in the group.

6. Insist on the Covenant. In the push to transform the church overnight into a network of Bible study and growth groups, the temptation will be to cut corners—especially on the requirements for membership in groups. Don't do it!

The Covenant at the beginning of each unit is there for a purpose. It gives each person a chance to commit himself/herself to the common disciplines of attendance, participation, confidentiality, accountability, etc. In the Advanced units, the Covenant also requires homework, shared responsibility for

leadership, and a commitment to reach out to others in a once-a-month "extended family" night.

If a person is unwilling to sign the Covenant, you should ask this person to wait until a later time when he/she is able to give himself/herself to the common disciplines.

7. Remember the empty chair. Even if you start groups with a general invitation for people to "sign up" at the beginning, keep an empty chair for people to enter the group after it has started.

Here you can decide on two policies: (a) allow people to enter at any time within a unit, or (b) allow people to enter only at the beginning of a new unit.

If you are already in the Advanced units, your group can decide to go back and do one or two of the Beginner sessions again — to give the newcomer a chance to get acquainted. Or, you can let the newcomer start where you are in the course.

8. After one year, REQUIRE that a group disband or come up with a good reason for continuing. From the very outset (before a group gets "so close" that they refuse to listen) explain that the group will last for ONE year . . . or two school years if you are taking off for summers.

If a group wishes to continue after this time, they MUST come back to the Leadership Team for assistance in developing a healthy, balanced programme of study and mission.

The Leadership Team, in turn, is responsible for directing the group into a new covenant — with a new purpose, study discipline, and mission.

9. Think about making study groups into "extended families" with the children. In the Advanced units, the Covenant already asks a group to get together once a month with spouses, kids, and "extended family." From this experience the concept of family clusters and caring units can be developed if the minister and elders/council of the church wish to move in this direction.

10. Start another Leadership Team. Eventually the original leadership team will not be enough to care for all of the new groups that want to start.

At this point the minister and elders/council will have to start a new Leadership Team and "shepherd" this team through the training.

This is the reason why the minister and elders/council need to be responsible ultimately for ALL the groups in the church. If Koinonia groups are meeting a need in the church, the minister needs to recognise this and multiply the groups. If the

Koinonia groups are becoming an ingrown "super spiritual" element within the church, the minister and elders/council should recognise this and stop the groups before further harm is done.

We are convinced that the Koinonia group model will prove to be the most effective tool for spiritual growth since the advent of the Sunday school class one hundred years ago.

GROUP SHARING
Groups of 2 / 20-25 Minutes

Planning Exercise

Leader: Make sure the group splits into pairs to work on this exercise. If there is an odd number, make one group of three. You may want to give out two sheets of blank paper to each person so that the notes can be kept private.

Instructions:
1. Divide into groups of 2.

2. Work with your partner on the strategy planning exercise on the next page. Don't worry about being completely accurate. The purpose of the exercise is to expand your consciousness about the potential in your church for Koinonia groups.

3. You will have approximately 20 minutes, and you do *not* have to finish the exercise.

SUMMING UP
All Together / 10-15 Minutes

Reporting In

Leader: Regather the class and ask each group of 2 to explain what they came up with in their planning exercise. Begin by asking each group to finish these two sentences and then explain.

☐ *We decided that the potential for Koinonia groups in our church is. . . .*

☐ *If we are going to penetrate every age level in our church with Koinonia groups, we need to. . . .*

☐ *If we are going to start these groups right, we need to. . . .*

PLANNING EXERCISE

This exercise is designed to help you think through the devlopment of Koinonia groups in your church. Listen to each other and explore each other's ideas—don't shoot each other down.

1. POTENTIAL POPULATION: Consider yourself a market analyst who has been asked to do an analysis of the potential for Koinonia groups in your church.

MEMBERSHIP: What is the maximum potential in your church for Koinonia groups?

☐ What is the membership of your church over 15 years of age?

_____

☐ How many people in your church are currently in Bible study/fellowship groups of any kind?

_____

☐ How many people are not involved in such a group?

_____

2. TARGET GROUPS: Using the categories below, decide in which areas of your church new Koinonia groups might be started. Tick the relevant box for each category.

	Groups already exist	Potential for new groups
Teenagers		
Young adults (18-25)		
Singles		
Young couples		
30-40 age		
40-50 age		
50+		
Other _____		

3. EXISTING GROUPS: List existing Bible study/fellowship groups in your church, and using the description of Koinonia groups (given on pages 16-17 "Theory Behind the Serendipity Group Model") rate them on the scale from 1 to 10. 1 = bear no resemblance to Koinonia groups; 10 = just like Koinonia groups as described.

List existing groups in your church	Rating
_____	1 _____ 5 _____ 10
_____	1 _____ 5 _____ 10
_____	1 _____ 5 _____ 10
_____	1 _____ 5 _____ 10
_____	1 _____ 5 _____ 10
_____	1 _____ 5 _____ 10
_____	1 _____ 5 _____ 10
_____	1 _____ 5 _____ 10
_____	1 _____ 5 _____ 10

Discuss together which units of this course would form a good starting place for existing groups. You may feel that some could start from scratch with Unit 1. Others may find it easier to start with Units 3-6.

4. PRE-START ANNOUNCEMENT, RECEPTION, REGISTRATION SCHEDULE FOR GROUPS: Now, think backward by six months and make a new timetable, indicating the start of the "whisper campaign," announcements, receptions, and group registration period.

SAMPLE (For the 6 months prior to the start of Bible study groups)

MAR	APR	MAY	JUNE	JULY	AUGUST	SEPT
Team Training			Whisper campaign*		Announcements	Receptions**

*Whisper campaign: Strategic leaks through the pastor, church staff, and Leadership Team that something "big" is about to be announced.

**Receptions: A carefully planned "in home" demonstration of what a Bible study group is all about — led by the Leadership Team — targeted to every age bracket — with someone in that age bracket "hosting" the occasion.

ROUGH CALENDAR OF EVENTS LEADING UP TO THE START OF BIBLE STUDY GROUPS

MARCH	APRIL	MAY	JUNE	JULY	AUGUST	SEPT

---

5. RECEPTIONS: When and where would you hold the crucial receptions for each age bracket, and WHO would you ask to be the host for each reception — someone who would do a bang-up job of getting people there.

TEENAGERS	YOUNG ADULTS	SINGLES	YOUNG COUPLES	AGES 30 TO 40	AGES 40 TO 50	OVER 50

---

6. TIMETABLE: Turn back to the schedule of this programme on page 4. Note the Beginning and Advanced units in this programme for Koinonia groups. Then create a timetable for nine months, showing how you would schedule Beginner groups and Advanced groups. (Remember, Beginner groups can choose one or both of the first two units — and run for 6 or 12 weeks.)

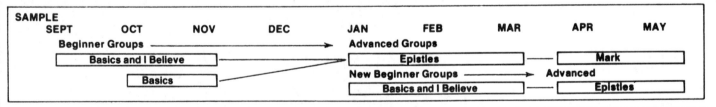

SAMPLE

SEPT	OCT	NOV	DEC	JAN	FEB	MAR	APR	MAY

Beginner Groups ————————————————→ Advanced Groups

Basics and I Believe ————→ Epistles — Mark

Basics

New Beginner Groups ————————→ Advanced

Basics and I Believe — Epistles

ROUGH CALENDAR FOR THE FIRST SCHOOL YEAR FOR BIBLE STUDY GROUPS

SEPT	OCT	NOV	DEC	JAN	FEB	MAR	APR	MAY

Note pages 38-39 for sample announcement, invitation, registration and covenant.

TRAINING

GROUP DISCIPLINES: Why do we need a group covenant?

Objectives: To have fun laughing about some of the problems in groups; to examine the group disciplines in the covenant; and to take inventory on your own group life in the last few weeks.

Setting: Small groups of 4 to 6.

Time: About 90 minutes

☐ Group Building Game / 25-30 Minutes

☐ Content / 15-20 Minutes

☐ Evaluation / 25-30 Minutes

☐ Summing Up / 10-15 Minutes

Materials required:

☐ Book and pencil for everyone

☐ One dice or spinner for each small group

Leadership: The leader must be familiar with the covenants at the beginning of each unit, especially the Beginner Group Covenant on page 42.

End result: At the conclusion of this session, the team should: (1) know what the group disciplines are all about, and (2) know how to evaluate a group from time to time for leadership skills.

GROUP BUILDING GAME
Groups of 4 to 6/25-30 Minutes

The Group Groans Game

Rationale: This game is based on the pitfalls that many groups fall into. If you can learn by the mistakes now, maybe you will not have to make all of the mistakes when you start groups in your church.

Instructions:

1. Each person selects a marker—a coin, key, lipstick container, etc., and places the marker on the starting line—like Monopoly.

2. One person (e.g., the person with the largest shoe size) begins the game by spinning the spinner or rolling dice and proceeding to that space on the game board.

GROUP

START

1. You start a whisper campaign about groups and everybody wants to join. SPIN AGAIN.

2. You schedule the orientation night during a sports special on T.V. No men show up. MISS A TURN.

3. You allow people to start a group without signing the covenant and some are half-hearted. GO BACK TO START.

4.

5. You skip the Beginner sessions and the group never gets acquainted. GO BACK 1 SPACE.

6.

7. Sam shares a problem he is having and you put it on the prayer chain. GO BACK 3 SPACES.

8.

9. You pray regularly for everyone in your group. MOVE AHEAD 3 SPACES.

10. Barb shares that her boyfriend is pressuring her to have sex. You pray about this and support her. MOVE AHEAD 1 SPACE.

11.

12. Sally comes to the meeting all upset. You take time to let her unload. ADVANCE 1 SPACE.

13.

14. It really is a BIG PROBLEM. You suggest the person go to the minister. MOVE AHEAD 2 SPACES FOR WISDOM.

15.

16. Bill shares his struggle with doubt and you lecture him for 15 minutes. GO BACK 2 SPACES FOR Information Overload.

The minister in your group asks for prayer for his problem with lust. You faint! GO BACK THREE SPACES FOR OVER REACTION.

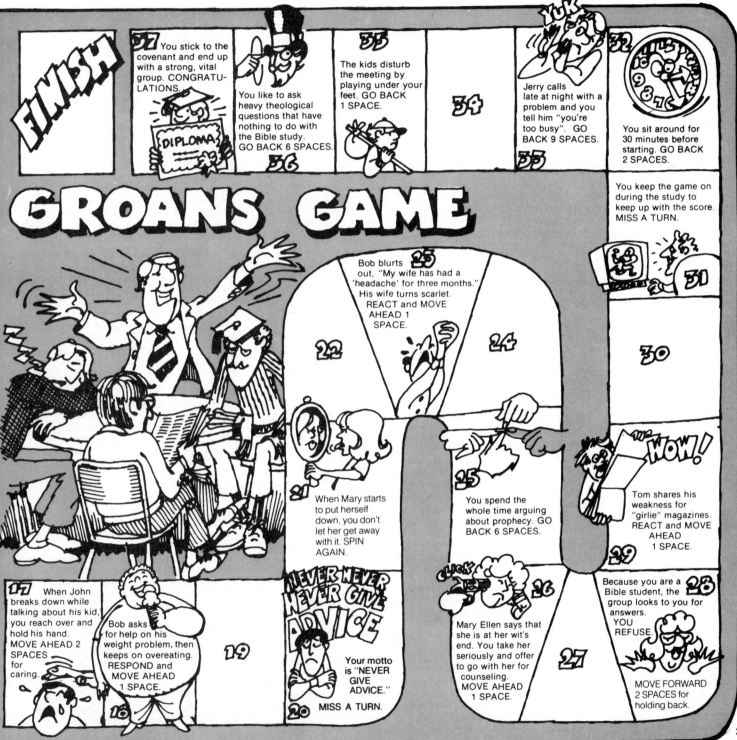

TRAINING

The person reads the space and responds accordingly.

3. The second person then makes his/her move. The game continues with players taking turns until one person "wins." To make it to the Finish Line, you must roll the exact number.

CONTENT
All Together/15-20 Minutes

The Group Covenant

Like weight watchers, a Bible study group needs a common discipline—a set of goals and agreements that everyone is committed to. Instead of a weight problem, these disciplines are designed to work on a spiritual growth problem—laziness, loneliness, and weakness.

In a Beginner group (Units I and/or II), the group must agree to six disciplines. In an Advanced group (beginning with Unit III), the group must agree to three more disciplines.

These disciplines form the basis for life together in the group. At the beginning of each unit the group renews the covenant. Anyone who feels they cannot agree to the minimum disciplines is allowed to get out—with honour. These nine disciplines are:

1. Attendance: "Priority is given to the group meetings. Except in case of emergency, you will be present and on time."

A Serendipity Bible study group is not for people who have it all together. It is for people who know they do *not* have it all together. For people who are struggling to make Jesus Christ the Lord of their lives, and readily admit that they cannot make it alone.

This first discipline is basic to all the others. To give priority to the weekly meeting means that you will be present unless an emergency comes up. If an emergency does come up, you will call someone in the group and tell this person why you cannot be there.

To safeguard the group from feeling tied down to this discipline, the covenant provides for an "exit" at the end of each unit—with honor. If you feel that you have other more pressing matters than the group meetings, you can drop out for a unit and come back when your schedule eases up.

2. Participation: The purpose of a group is to become a group—to become a spiritual faith community. In the first two units, everyone tells the story of their "faith journey" to the group.

It is only as we "tell our story" that people can identify with us. Reach out. Care. Experience what the New Testament calls "koinonia"—

oneness in the common bond of our faith journey and struggles.

This is why the second discipline is so important. To agree to be in a group is to agree to participate—to open up your life, your story, your struggles—and let the group be a part of this story.

3. Confidentiality: "Anything that is shared in the group is kept in strict confidence." This is not a therapy group, but information will be shared from time to time that should not be repeated outside the group.

The biggest drawback to sharing in a Bible study group is the fear that someone in the group will "blab" what you said around the church. The person may be harmed. The group may be harmed because it will cease to be a place where you can come with your problems.

4. Accountability: At the close of every session, an opportunity is given to share new goals you want to set for your life. When you state a new goal and ask the others in the group to support you in this goal, you are giving permission to the group to hold you accountable.

This discipline does *not* apply to needs that you have not shared. For instance, a person does *not* have the right to ask you, "How are you doing with your wife," if you have not shared this as a problem. Accountability is not prying into your life. Accountability is holding you to the things where you have asked the group for support.

5. Accessability: This is the other side of accountability. Here you give permission to the members of your group to call you when they have a problem—even at 3 o'clock in the morning. In fact, the 3 o'clock in the morning permission is exactly what is required if a group is going to be serious about their commitment to one another.

If you know anything about Alcoholics Anonymous, you know what we mean by this discipline. Somehow, we need to learn how to apply the same model to those who know they are spiritually weak, lonely, and vulnerable to temptation.

6. Evangelisation: The group is willing and ready at any time to adopt a person who needs the support and correction of your group. In forming a group, you agree to keep an "empty chair" for anyone who needs your help and is willing to agree to the disciplines.

The temptation in a small caring group is to resist letting anyone else in. "If so and so joins us *now*, he/she will *ruin* our closeness." This is possibly true, but the opposite of this is worse—an ingrown, spiritual clique—masquerading as a Bible study group.

When a new person comes in, you may have

to spend a week or so retelling your "stories." (The Spiritual Pilgrimage exercise on page 147 would be a great session for this.) If your group already has 7 or 8, you can split up into two rooms when the time comes for sharing—4 around the dining table and 4 around the kitchen table, etc. When you have too many to meet in one house, split the group into two houses. But don't close the door to someone who needs you.

7. Homework: (When you get to Unit III, the group must agree to three more disciplines). The homework discipline requires that you complete the Bible study assignment before you get to the group meeting.

The homework can be done in one sitting, but it is recommended that the assignment be spread over three or four days—giving you something to work on each day in your personal devotions.

8. Shared Leadership: After the first two units, the group assumes responsibility for its own leadership. This means that you agree to rotate the leadership around the group—a different person leading each week.

Sharing Questions at the side of the worksheet for each session makes the leading easy. But there is still need for a referee to blow the whistle from time to time and bring the discussion back to the lesson—and moving through the worksheet.

9. Monthly Outreach: This discipline is to focus on the missing people in the group—your spouses, children, and extended family. Too often, someone gets left out when you get involved in a Bible study group. Sometimes those left out feel resentful, particularly if you come home and talk about the good time you are having. Or, because they are not invited, they are not interested in hearing you talk about the good time you are having.

All of this can be changed if you make your family members feel a part of your Koinonia group. This is the reason for the once-a-month social get-together.

Hopefully, as your spouses and kids get acquainted with each other, your social evenings will evolve into deeper fellowship, outings, picnics, camping trips, Christmas parties, and old-fashioned family reunions.

GROUP SHARING
Same Groups as Game/25-30 Minutes

Evaluation

Leader: The Evaluation questionnaire below is actually for evaluating groups later on. We suggest you use it now to become familiar with the tool and to raise any questions about the Covenant and leadership skills by diagnosing your own training group experience.

Instructions:

1. In silence complete the Evaluation questionnaire below. The questionnaire is designed for a regular Bible study group after *each* unit. As you fill in the questionnaire, apply the questions to the leadership team that you have been a part of.

Pause for 3 or 4 minutes. Then, call time and proceed.

2. Regather with the small group that you were with in the Game.

3. In GROUP DISCIPLINES, discuss *only* those points which you circled from 1 to 5 — indicating that you have or might have a problem with this.

4. Go around a second time on the COMMUNICATION ASSIGNMENT. Discuss only the statements where you indicated a question or problem.

5. On the LEADERSHIP ASSESSMENT, share only the statements where you checked, "Sorry you asked."

6. On RECOMMENDATIONS, focus on ways you could strengthen or make the Covenant more

relevant to your own particular church situation.

**SUMMING UP
All Together/10-15 Minutes**

Reporting In

Leader: Gather everyone together. Ask someone from each group to summarize the recommendations that came out of the group sharing. Ask for questions, especially about the Covenant.

Deal with any business and close in prayer.

EVALUATION: From time to time the group should stop and check to see if their health is good as a group. This little self inventory questionnaire is designed to help you in this process. After you have completed the questionnaire in silence, get together in groups and share your results.

GROUP DISCIPLINES: Rank your group performance against the spiritual disciplines of the group covenant. Circle a number from 1 to 10 — 1 being poor performance and 10 being an excellent performance.

Attendance: We give priority to group meetings except in case of emergency.
1   2   3   4   5   6   7   8   9   10

Participation: Everyone has been able to participate in the sharing.
1   2   3   4   5   6   7   8   9   10

Confidentiality: We keep everything that is shared in confidence.
1   2   3   4   5   6   7   8   9   10

Accountability: When someone shares a goal, we support this person and hold this person accountable to do what he/she says he will do.
1   2   3   4   5   6   7   8   9   10

Accessability: We call upon each other in times of personal need—even in the middle of the night.
1   2   3   4   5   6   7   8   9   10

Evangelisation: We reach out to others who need a group for spiritual support.
1   2   3   4   5   6   7   8   9   10

Homework: We have completed our Bible study assignment before the meeting.
1   2   3   4   5   6   7   8   9   10

Shared Leadership: We rotate the responsibility for leadership.
1   2   3   4   5   6   7   8   9   10

Outreach: We get together at least once a month with our spouses, kids, and extended family.
1   2   3   4   5   6   7   8   9   10

COMMUNICATION ASSESSMENT: Evaluate your group on these communication principles: Put a dot on the line—somewhere in between ALWAYS and NEVER for each of these statements.

	ALWAYS	NEVER
We respect each other's opinions.		
We concentrate on listening well.		
We are not afraid of feelings.		
We seek to affirm each other . . . where we are.		
We refrain from giving advice.		
We avoid mental exercise and verbal gymnastics.		
We give priority to anyone who needs to unload.		

LEADERSHIP ASSESSMENT: Rate your group leadership quotient on these basic areas. Tick a box after each statement to indicate your response.

EVERY TIME	MOST OF THE TIME	SORRY YOU ASKED	
☐	☐	☐	The physical setting is very conducive for sharing.
☐	☐	☐	We start and end on time.
☐	☐	☐	We stick to the Bible study unless someone needs to share.
☐	☐	☐	We cover the Bible study worksheet, including Application.
☐	☐	☐	Everyone participates and no one too much.
☐	☐	☐	We keep an empty chair for newcomers.
☐	☐	☐	The leader sets the pace for transparency and openness.
☐	☐	☐	We have a clearly defined purpose and everybody is committed to this purpose.

RECOMMENDATIONS: To improve our group, what recommendations would you propose?

1. Do we need to amend the covenant? If so, where?

2. Do we need to add anything to the covenant? If so, what?

3. In the next unit, what do we need to work on in our life together?

TRAINING

LEADERSHIP TEAM: Where do I fit in?

Objective: To examine your spiritual gifts; to figure out who fits where in the Leadership Team responsibilities; to decide if you wish to be on the Leadership Team; to decide how to proceed; to celebrate your experience.

Setting: Groups of 6 to 8—with people who know each other well.

Materials required:

☐ Book and pencil for everyone

☐ **BIBLES** for everyone

☐ Spinner or dice for each group of 4

☐ Refreshments for party afterward

Leadership: The Coordinator who is in charge of ALL groups should lead this session. The Coordinator must know what the minister and elders/council of the church are willing to go along with on developing a network of Koinonia groups. The Coordinator should be familiar with the options on pages 38-39 for expanding the Koinonia groups into on-going "caring units."

End result: At the conclusion of this session, the team should: (1) understand the biblical concept of gifts, (2) know some of their own gifts, (3) know their own role on the Leadership Team, and (4) be enthusiastic about it.

GROUP BUILDING GAME
Groups of 6 to 8/20 to 30 Minutes

Wedding At Cana

Rationale: Specific responsibilities for the small Koinonia groups in your church will rest on the shoulders of the Leadership Team. The Leadership Team will have to divide up the chores for administering these groups. The best

way to divide up the work is to figure out your spiritual gifts and assign the work according to your specific gifts. This game will help you to recognise the spiritual gifts in each other.

Instructions:

1. *Step One:* Give a Bible to everyone or read the Bible story aloud to everyone—John 2:1-11

2. *Step Two:* Go back to the cartoon of this story and try to identify the various people in the story with the personalities of the people in your group; for instance, who in your group is good at:

   ☐ Hospitality: "Please, enjoy our house, you are welcome...."

   ☐ Generosity/giving: "I want to give you these jars for your wine...."

   ☐ Recognising a problem before it gets bad: "We have a problem here...."

   ☐ Doing something about a problem: "Do whatever he tells you...."

   ☐ Giving spiritual direction: "Fill the jars with water...."

   ☐ Encouraging: "Please don't get discouraged. I'm sure the problem will be taken care of...."

   ☐ Helping: "Here, let me help you with those jars...."

Leader: Pause 3 or 4 minutes in silence for everyone to identify the others in the Bible story with the personalities of those in the group. If they are having trouble, give an example of the person you identify with ... and how you would identify one or two others in your group with people in the story.

3. *Step Three:* One person sits in silence while the others in the group explain how they would identify this person with someone in the Bible story.

   Then, ask another person to sit in silence while the others explain how they would identify this person with someone in the story, etc.

   Continue this procedure until everyone in the group has been "affirmed" in this way.

BIBLE STUDY
Same Groups/20-30 Minutes

Leader: This Bible study is in two parts: (1) Silent preparation, and (2) Sharing in groups. EVERYONE WILL NEED A BIBLE. You can use any translation, preferably a modern translation that expands on the words for the various "spiritual gifts" in Romans 12:6-8.

1. Silent Preparation: Open your Bibles to Romans 12 and complete the questions. (If you have time, refer to the two other Scripture passages on spiritual gifts: Ephesians 4:11-13 and 1 Corinthians 12.)

2. Focusing on Romans 12:1-11, answer the following questions:

   a. What is the basic preparation for finding out your spiritual gift? (Romans 12:1-2)

   b. How can you be better prepared?

   c. What are the basic attitudes regarding the use of gifts? (Romans 12:3-6a)

   d. What gifts are mentioned in Romans 12:6b-11? In the middle column you will find a brief definition for eight spiritual gifts found in Romans 12. In the left column, jot down the "gift" that goes with the definition. In the right column, jot down a character in the Wedding at Cana story that comes the closest to this gift.

GIFT	MEANING	CHARACTER
Prophecy	One who speaks God's word to a specific situation, forthright and uncompromising.	Jesus
	One who is good at giving encouragement, challenge and exortation—a natural born football team coach.	
	One who is good at setting goals and organising others to meet these goals—a true administrator.	
	One who is good at meeting practical needs—super conscientious and faithful.	
	One who is good at caring when somebody is hurting—compassionate and super sensitive.	
	One who is good at communicating ideas and making the Scripture understandable to others.	
	One who is good in financial matters and long-range strategy, investment, and management of resources for the cause of Christ.	

Leader: If your group is unfamiliar with the meaning of the words for spiritual gifts in Romans 12:6-8, it will be necessary for you to do a word study on these words before the session.

3. Group Sharing. Regather in the same groups that you were in for the Game.

4. Go around and share the results of the Bible study . . . "a" through "d." Then, explain how you matched the definitions for various spiritual gifts with the words in Romans 12:6-8.
   Then, discuss how you matched the spiritual gifts in the Scripture with various people in the Bible story—the Wedding at Cana.

TEAM ASSIGNMENTS
All Together / 20-30 Minutes

Sharing My Gift

Leader: Before the session you need to make a list of all of the responsibilities that are needed to develop a TOTAL Koinonia group programme in your church. If the list below is not complete, add the jobs that we have left out. On the other hand, if you are going to begin with only one or two groups, you may not need all of these jobs now.

1. In silence, read over the partial list of jobs that are needed to develop a full Bible study group ministry in a church. Check two or three items on this list where you feel you would be suited best because of your "spiritual gift." Be honest.

____ Minister: As the spiritual director of the church, the minister must be involved in the programme, including the final selection of all team personnel.

____ Deacons/Elders: This official body needs to approve the concept of Koinonia groups and to be represented on the team.

____ Director: With the gift of prophet, teacher, and exhorter, this person needs to be a born team leader—strong salesman, coach, and motivator.

____ Administrator: With the gift of organisation, administration, and helping, this person needs to be good at details, follow through, and behind-the-scenes hard work.

____ Communicator: With the gift of communication (speaking, writing, or advertising), this person needs to translate the dream of Koinonia groups throughout the church into well planned and well produced promotional campaigns, with *enticing* announcements for the minister to give, in the church paper, and on the church notice board.

____ Group Leaders: With the gifts of sharing, caring, listening, enabling, and encouraging, these persons are needed as leaders of every Beginner Koinonia group for the first few weeks.

____ Mission Coordinator: With the gifts of compassion, healthy discontent, and a driving zeal to reach out to the lonely "prodigal" spiritual drop-outs in the church . . . that probably will NOT be drawn into groups unless someone reaches out to them. (The danger of any Bible study group programme is that it does not reach the people on the fringe of the church who need it most.)

2. Regather as a group—all together. Go around and finish these two sentences:

   ☐ My dream for our church as far as Koinonia groups are concerned is to . . .

   ☐ To see this dream become a reality, I am prepared to . . . .

3. Brainstorm as a group on each of these questions:

   ☐ What does God want our church to be?

   ☐ What can we do to help make this kind of church become a reality?

   ☐ How do we get started?

SUMMING UP
All Together / 10 Minutes

Hour of Decision

Leader: At the close ask for a commitment to be on the Leadership Team. Remind the Team of the THREE priorities:

☐ **Priority # 1:** *To give priority to your own spiritual growth—to meet weekly for Bible study, prayer, and mutual support.*

☐ **Priority # 2:** *To give priority to the particular mission of developing Koinonia groups in your church—to contribute your spiritual gift in whatever capacity God leads you to share.*

☐ **Priority # 3:** *To give priority to the on-going life and mission of the church—to support the overall programme and the minister in whatever way you can.*

If you have not signed the LEADERSHIP TEAM LIST on page 40, ask those who are willing to serve on the Leadership Team to sign each other's books as a token of their commitment.

A WORD TO MINISTERS AND RELIGIOUS EDUCATORS

There is no doctrinal, denominational, or theological slant in this course. The approach to Scripture is basically "devotional," allowing each person to record his or her "meditation" upon a Bible passage.

☐ In the first few weeks (Units I or II), the group sharing is based on group-building conversation starters and relational Bible study—which allows a person to "tell their story" to the group.

☐ After a "trial" period, the group moves to the Advanced units III, IV, V, and VI (available from Scripture Union).

☐ In the Advanced units, the Bible study assignment is completed before the group session.

☐ A blank worksheet is filled out for the Bible study homework assignment.

☐ The blank worksheet is the basis for the group sharing at the meetings.

☐ There are Sharing Questions for every session—next to the worksheet.

☐ Group members are encouraged to use outside Bible study resources in their study at home, but not to bring these to meetings.

☐ In the Beginner groups, a leader is assigned from the Leadership Team. After this, the leadership rotates within the group.

☐ Ministers, religious educators, and teachers are encouraged to join in the groups, but not to exercise authoritarian control.

☐ Three safeguards have been built into the course: (1) a "trial" period with a trained group leader, (2) structured agenda for each session, and (3) specific covenants for groups to sign at the beginning of each unit.

☐ Once a month, the group is asked to invite their spouses, children, and "extended family" to a fun evening. Programmes for these get-togethers are on pages 73-95.

ANNOUNCEMENT

KOINONIA GROUPS: Our church will be initiating a number of small groups this _____ (season) for those who know they need a little help in their spiritual growth.

CHRISTIAN WEIGHT WATCHERS GROUP: The programme works like Weight Watchers. You sign up for a specific period of weeks . . . and meet as a group with others who know they need support and encouragement. Together you agree to these disciplines:

- ☐ to meet once a week
- ☐ to share the story of your spiritual journey with one another
- ☐ to study the Bible
- ☐ to pray for each other
- ☐ to call upon each other when you feel down or spiritually low
- ☐ to reach out to others who are struggling

AFTER A "TRIAL" PERIOD, A MORE SERIOUS COVENANT: A Beginner group can last from 6 to 12 weeks (depending upon the group). After this time, the group can sign up for an Advanced program for up to 40 more weeks. In addition to the Beginner disciplines, an Advanced group agrees:

- ☐ to spend a little time every day in the study of Scripture and to complete a worksheet of your Bible study for discussion at the group meetings
- ☐ to share in leading the group—using the "sharing questions" that are provided in the program
- ☐ to get together once a month with all of your spouses and kids as a family cluster

HOW TO FIND OUT MORE: A series of first nights are being held at homes during the week of _____ for those who want to know more about this programme. The first nights will be held at:

Night:_____ Host:_____ Phone: _____

Night:_____ Host:_____ Phone: _____

Night:_____ Host:_____ Phone: _____

Night:_____ Host:_____ Phone: _____

IF YOU'RE "TOO BUSY," YOU NEED TO SAY "YES": If you are struggling to maintain a spiritual discipline and think you are too busy to get into a group, YOU are the person this programme is designed for. YOU probably eat breakfast anyway. Why not join a Koinonia group for breakfast, coffee, or lunch, and use your time DOUBLE.

INVITATION TO FIRST NIGHTS

You are invited
to attend a first night

at the home of _____ (host)

on the evening of _____ (date).

The purpose of the first night is to acquaint you with the programme for Koinonia groups in our church.

_____

and

_____

(names of Leadership Team members)
will introduce the idea of a Christian
"weight watchers" group
for people who need a little
support from a group
in spiritual growth disciplines.

The first group meeting will be over breakfast/coffee/lunch.

Sign up for the group of your choice and convenience.

R.S.V.P.

_____ (name) _____ (phone)

_____ (name) _____ (phone)

_____ (name) _____ (phone)

REGISTRATION

Koinonia Group

Now is the time to sign up for a Koinonia group. The groups, which will start on the week of _____, are designed for those who know they need a little support in their spiritual growth disciplines.

Like Weight Watchers, you agree to keep a spiritual discipline for a "trial" period of 6 to 12 weeks:

☐ to meet once a week as a group

☐ to share the story of your spiritual journey with one another

☐ to study the Bible

☐ to pray for each other

☐ to call upon each other when you feel down or spiritually low

☐ to reach out to others who need you

Groups will be offered for all age brackets . . . and scheduled to meet throughout the week over breakfast, coffee, lunch, or in the evening.

PLEASE INDICATE WHICH GROUP YOU WOULD BE INTERESTED IN:

☐ Early morning MEN'S group (breakfast) on _____ (day)

☐ Mid-morning WOMEN'S group (coffee) on _____ (day)

☐ Saturday morning MEN'S group

☐ YOUNG ADULT evening group on _____ (day)

☐ YOUNG COUPLE'S evening group on _____ (day)

☐ COUPLE'S group on _____ (day)

☐ MIXED Sunday night group

Name _____

Address _____

_____

Phone _____

I understand this is a 6 or 12 week commitment to a "trial" group experience and I agree to give priority to the meetings of this group.

Signed _____

COVENANT

Beginner Koinonia Group

This is an agreement for a Beginner Koinonia group. The spiritual disciplines set forth in this agreement are designed to foster the spiritual growth and maturity of each person.

This agreement is for a period of 6 or 12 weeks. (Tick under 'Organisation.') During this "trial" period, it is understood that you will give priority to this group and will endeavour to carry out the agreements set forth in this covenant.

☐ *Attendance:* to meet once a week

☐ *Participation:* to share your spiritual "story" with each other through Bible study and open-ended questions

☐ *Confidentiality:* to hold in strict confidence anything that is shared within the group

☐ *Accountability:* to support one another in any goals you set for yourself

☐ *Accessibility:* to be available to each other in times of spiritual need—even in the middle of the night

☐ *Evangelisation:* to reach out to others who need your group

If you decide to continue as a group after the "trial" period, you must renew this Covenant and add three more spiritual disciplines.

ORGANISATION

Duration: We will meet for (tick one):   ☐ 6 weeks   ☐ 12 weeks

Place: We will meet at _____

Time: We will meet from _____ to _____

Refreshments: We will serve _____

Babysitting: _____

I will try with God's help to be a regular, faithful, caring member of this group.

Signed _____

NAMES OF GROUP MEMBERS	PHONE
_____	_____
_____	_____
_____	_____
_____	_____
_____	_____
_____	_____

Leadership Team List

Name _____

Address _____

_____ Code _____

Telephone _____

Name _____

Address _____

_____ Code _____

Telephone _____

Name _____

Address _____

_____ Code _____

Telephone _____

Name _____

Address _____

_____ Code _____

Telephone _____

Name _____

Address _____

_____ Code _____

Telephone _____

Name _____

Address _____

_____ Code _____

Telephone _____

Name _____

Address _____

_____ Code _____

Telephone _____

Name _____

Address _____

_____ Code _____

Telephone _____

Name _____

Address _____

_____ Code _____

Telephone _____

Name _____

Address _____

_____ Code _____

Telephone _____

Basics

BOOK ONE

6 SESSIONS TO BECOME A GROUP THAT CARES

*This is one of two courses used for introducing
small groups to Serendipity. Choose one or both.
Before you start on this course, make sure that everyone in the
group is committed to the covenant on the next page.*

WHY SIGN A COVENANT?

Before you start on this course, it is important to agree as a group on your goals and common disciplines. Like Weight Watchers, the strength of the group is in the common disciplines.

You can agree to meet for 6 sessions (Unit I) or for 12 sessions (Units I and II), with these minimum disciplines. (Units I and II are both "Beginner" courses suitable for new groups, or groups who have not used Serendipity before.)

1. Attendance: Priority is given to the group meetings. Except in case of emergency, you will be present and on time.

2. Participation: The purpose of the first 6 sessions is to get acquainted and build a sense of oneness, or "koinonia," in your group. This is accomplished by letting each group member "tell his or her spiritual story" to the group. To be in a group, you must be willing to let the group hear "your story."

3. Confidentiality: Anything that is shared in the group is kept in strict confidence. This is not a therapy group, but information will be shared from time to time that should not be repeated outside the group.

4. Accountability: At the close of every session, an opportunity is given for you to share new goals you want to set for your life. When you state a goal and ask the others in the group to "support" you in these goals, you are giving permission to the group to "hold you accountable."

5. Accessibility: The group is for people who *know* they are weak and *need* the help of others to overcome temptation, spiritual depression, and chronic weakness. In asking to be in a group, you are admitting you need support . . . and that you are willing to support others in the same condition.
   To be in a group, you are giving others permission to call on you for spiritual help — even at three o'clock in the morning — and you are asking for the same permission from others.

6. Evangelisation: The group is willing and ready at any time to adopt new people who need the support and correction of your group. In forming a group, you also agree to "keep an empty chair" for anyone who needs your help and is willing to agree to these minimum disciplines.

BEGINNER GROUP COVENANT

For the next 6 weeks, we agree to the following disciplines as a group.

☐ Attendance: To give priority to the group meetings.

☐ Participation: To give ourselves to the purpose of the group — to get to know each other by sharing our spiritual journeys with one another.

☐ Confidentiality: To keep anything that is shared strictly confidential.

☐ Accountability: To allow the rest of the group to hold each of us accountable for goals *we* set for *ourselves.*

☐ Accessibility: To give each other the right to call upon one another for spiritual help in times of temptation and need — even in the middle of the night.

☐ Evangelisation: To keep the door to our group *open* to others in our church who need help.

SPECIFICS:

We will meet on _____ (day of week).

We will meet at _____ (home/place).

The meeting will begin at _____ and close at _____.

ORGANISATION: What do we want to do about . . .

☐ Refreshments: _____

☐ Baby-sitting: _____

☐ Newcomers: _____

☐ Absence: _____

I will try with God's help to be a regular, faithful, caring member of this group.

Signed: _____

NAMES OF GROUP MEMBERS	PHONE

As new people join the group, add their names to this list. REMEMBER, NEW PEOPLE CAN ENTER THE GROUP AT ANY TIME IN THE COURSE.

BASICS: A GUIDE TO THE COURSE

1 Getting to Know Each Other

ICE BREAKER
Option 1
FOUR QUAKER QUESTIONS
Where were you living between the ages of 7 and 12 and what were the winters like? Each person to explain.
Option 2
MY WORLD
Pinpoint these significant spots: where you were born, most memorable holiday, honeymoon spot, retirement dream.

RELATIONAL BIBLE STUDY
The Odd Couple
Listen in on this little "fuss" between two sisters — Mary and Martha — and choose which one you would rather have for a roommate. For a close friend. To be executor of your will. To go to when you have a problem. To work for. To work for you. For a next-door neighbour, etc. Through this Bible story, explain a little about yourself, eg. what you want/need to get out of this Bible study group, and what Jesus might tell you if he "dropped in" on your house.

2 Our Spiritual Beginnings

ICE BREAKER
Personal Scavenger Hunt
Take a quick scavenger hunt through your handbag, pockets, or clothes and find four items: (a) Something I prize/cherish, (b) Something that gives me pleasure, (c) Something that gives me concern, and (d) Something that reveals a lot about me. "Show and tell" these four items with your Bible study group and share some of the important things about yourself that your group needs to know.

RELATIONAL BIBLE STUDY
The Fisherman That Got Hooked
Walk through the story of Simon Peter — when Jesus invited him to "put out into deep water and let down the nets for a catch." Compare your own early memories of meeting Jesus Christ to Simon Peter's story, and share the similarities and differences between your story and Simon's story. What is the "deep water" for you right now? Where is Jesus asking you to risk "getting your nets wet"? This is a very important session for your group.

3 Growing Through Difficulties

ICE BREAKER
Music in My Life
In your personal life, are you feeling more like "Blues in the Night" or "Feeling Groovy"? In your family life, are you feeling more like "Stormy Weather" or "The Sound of Music"? In your work or career, are you feeling more like "Take This Job and Shove It" or "Everything's Coming Up Roses"? In your spiritual life, are you feeling more like "The Dead March" or "Hallelujah Chorus"? Here's a chance to use music to describe a little about how you're feeling.

RELATIONAL BIBLE STUDY
Stormy Weather
It all started out as a quiet, peaceful, much deserved night off for the disciples, but something happened. Read the story of "the storm" and compare some of the "storms" that have come into your life and how you are reacting to the "weather" right now. What do the words of Jesus mean for you right now: "Quiet! Be still!"? Here's a chance to share some of the struggles that you might be going through . . . and what God is saying.

4 Happiness is

ICE BREAKER
The Four Temperaments
Hippocrates, hundreds of years before Christ, described four basic personality types: (a) Sanguine, (b) Choleric, (c) Melancholic, and (d) Phlegmatic. Decide which temperament best describes you. (Hint: you can be a little bit of two or three.)

RELATIONAL BIBLE STUDY
The Beatitudes
What are the characteristics of a person who wishes to be a follower of Jesus Christ? Jesus explained these in the Sermon on the Mount. Measure your own "mental attitude" against this list and score yourself from 1 to 4 on each beatitude. Then, when you share, reverse the process and let the others in your group "affirm" the Beatitudes they see in your life. You may be surprised to discover that your group sees many more strengths in your life than you do.

5 Asking and Receiving

ICE BREAKER
Stress Test
Take the test that Dr. Richard Rahe developed to find out how many stress points you have right now in your life. One hundred and fifty is a maximum, and most of us are living beyond this limit. When you have added up your score, compare results. This could be valuable for yourself . . . and for the others in your group.

RELATIONAL BIBLE STUDY
Three Parables on Prayer
Jesus didn't talk very much about prayer. And when he did, it was often in parables. Look at three of these parables and see if you can find a common thread that runs through these stories. This is going to get you talking about some of your own concepts of God, of what he wants out of you, and what you need to do to draw on his resources. It is also going to let you share what you see as the next "scary" step in your faith journey, and pray together about it.

6 Becoming a Group that Cares

ICE BREAKER
I Predict
Here's your chance to make some famous predictions about the people in your group. Who is likely to be the first woman to win the Grand National? Who is likely to be a world famous hairdresser? Who is likely to write an advice column for the lovelorn? Here's your chance to get back at your buddies and get ready for a lovely wrap-up to this course.

RELATIONAL BIBLE STUDY
The Jesus Pattern
In an age of "top dog" executive management, the pattern that Jesus gave to his disciples for "true greatness" may appear a little old-fashioned. Walk through this story of Jesus "washing the feet" of his disciples and see if there is anything here for you and your group. Then, give each one a chance to share what this group has meant to you . . . and what you would like to do to move on.

INTRODUCTION

RATIONALE: In the first session of any group, you need to spend most of the time getting acquainted—telling a little about yourself, why you are here, and what you hope to get out of the group. The Relational Bible Study is designed for this.

AGENDA: This session is divided into three parts:

(1) Ice Breaker / 10 Minutes

(2) Relational Bible Study / 40 Minutes

(3) Signing the Covenant / 10 Minutes

LEADER: Follow the "check list" on the opposite page for further instructions. Be sure to save time at the close to discuss and sign the covenant for the next 6 weeks. Be sure you have a book for everyone. This is very important.

ICE BREAKER/10 Minutes

Before you move into the Bible study, we suggest that you take a few minutes to get acquainted. Move your chairs into small clusters of 4 or 5 each, such as 4 people around the dining table, 4 around the kitchen table and 4 around the coffee table. Then, introduce this fun ice breaker.

Option 1
FOUR QUAKER QUESTIONS

Here are four questions that let you get into the significant childhood memories of your life. Go around your group of 4 on the first question. Then, go around again on the second question, etc.

1. **Where were you living between the ages of 7 and 12 . . . and what were the winters like?**

2. **How did you heat your house during this time?**

3. **What was the center of warmth in your life during this time? (This can be a place in the house, a time of year or a person).**

4. **When did God become a "warm" person to you and how did it happen?**

Option 2
MY WORLD

Pinpoint these significant places:
- ☐ **where I was born**
- ☐ **most memorable holiday**
- ☐ **my dream honeymoon spot**
- ☐ **where I would choose to live**

Getting to Know Each Other

Goal: To get to know a few other people better than you did before, to share a little about yourself by walking through a "story" in Scripture and showing how this story relates to your own life, to find out more about the "spiritual disciplines" in the group covenant, and to start the process of building a spiritual "weight watchers" support group.

RELATIONAL BIBLE STUDY
The Odd Couple

Listen in on this little "kitchen incident" in Scripture and use this experience to share a little about yourself with the group. In this study, you do not have to wait to fill out the questionnaire before starting to share. Just have the first person in your group "choose between" Mary or Martha "As a roommate." Then, the next person choose between Mary

or Martha "For a close friend," etc.

When you get to MY OWN STORY, slow down and have each person explain their answer for the first question. Then, go around again on the second question, etc.

Be sure to save time at the close to DISCUSS and SIGN the Covenant on page 42.

> *As Jesus and his disciples were on their way, he came to a village where a woman named Martha opened her home to him. She had a sister called Mary, who sat at the Lord's feet listening to what he said. But Martha was distracted by all the preparations that had to be made. She came to him and asked, "Lord, don't you care that my sister has left me to do the work by myself? Tell her to help me!"*
>
> *"Martha, Martha," the Lord answered, "you are worried and upset about many things, but only one thing is needed. Mary has chosen what is better, and it will not be taken away from her."*
>
> Luke 10:38-42 NIV

IF I HAD TO CHOOSE: If you had to choose between Mary and Martha in the following situations, which would you choose (tick one):

MARY	MARTHA		MARY	MARTHA	
☐	☐	As a roommate	☐	☐	To work for
☐	☐	For a close friend	☐	☐	To work for me
☐	☐	To be executor of my will	☐	☐	To be my next-door neighbour
☐	☐	To go to when I have a problem	☐	☐	To be my pastor

I AM SOMEWHERE BETWEEN: Put a dot on the line on each category to indicate how you see yourself. For Example:

On Housework, I am....
Dirty dishes everywhere — Slippers at the door
Mary _____ Martha

On Temperament, I am....
Easy going — Explosive
Mary _____ Martha

On Taking Responsibility, I am....
Little sister — Take charge
Mary _____ Martha

On Spiritual Priorities, I am....
Guilty if I don't start
the day with God
Mary _____

Doing well if I open
the Bible once a week
_____Martha

On Dealing with Sour Relationships at Home, I am ...
Sweep it under the carpet
Mary _____

Let's have it out now
_____Martha

On Organizing My Life, I am ...
Too heavenly minded
Mary _____

A stitch in time saves nine
_____Martha

Looking into the Story

Go around and have each person share their response to these questions—one question at a time.

1. Why do you think Jesus went to Mary and Martha's home?
a. they were close friends
b. he had nowhere else to go
c. he needed their fellowship
d. he wanted to help Mary
e. he wanted to help Martha
f. other _____

2. What do you think Jesus meant when he said to Martha that *"Mary has chosen what is better"?*
a. she needed to get her priorities straightened out
b. people are more important than a nice home
c. spiritual fellowship is more important than food
d. fussing over little things is a sign of spiritual immaturity
e. people who let their housework go are more spiritual
f. other _____

3. If you had been Martha, how would you have responded to Jesus' remarks?
a. flown off the handle
b. been embarrassed
c. thought to myself, "Who does he think he is to tell me how to be a hostess?"
d. accepted the rebuke
e. gone to my bedroom and cried
f. sat down with Jesus and let the supper burn
g. other _____

4. Why do you think Jesus said what he did to Martha?
a. she was picking on her little sister
b. she was getting on his nerves
c. he knew her well enough to say this without hurting her

d. he really wanted to help her rearrange her priorities
e. he enjoyed putting people down
f. he knew that he had only one more week to live and he wanted to spend the time with her

My Own Story

1. If Jesus dropped in on you today at your house, what would be two or three things he would recommend? (List top 3)
____ turn down the music
____ turn off the TV
____ reorganize your time
____ go to bed earlier
____ set aside time every day with him
____ slow down and enjoy life
____ take some time off to find out what's important
____ spend more time with your family
____ get off your backside and start ____

2. The idea of opening up and sharing some of my struggles with this Bible study group sounds:
a. risky
b. strange
c. dangerous
d. valuable, but
e. okay, if everybody else will
f. just what I'm looking for
g. ask me next week

3. If this Bible study group really wants to help me in my spiritual growth, they need to:
a. hold me to my spiritual commitment
b. be very gentle with me
c. be open about their own struggles
d. give me a good kick in the pants when I need it
e. keep praying for me
f. other _____

CHECKLIST FOR THE LEADER

BEFORE THE SESSION

☐ Coordinator: This Bible study programme needs supervision. Before starting any group, equip some group leaders by using the 6 Sessions to train your leadership team in the Leader's Guide.

☐ Group Leaders: Continue to meet with your Coordinator (even after the training programme is over) for your own spiritual support. At the meeting, spend about half of the time on your own needs and half on planning the session.

☐ Room: Choose a house or place where you can split into smaller groups—4 to 5 people per group—when the time comes for sharing, such as 4 or 5 at the kitchen table, 4 or 5 at the dining table, etc. Keep the groups small ... and always draw up an empty chair to remind you that there is always room for one more at the next meeting.

☐ Agenda: Divide the time into three parts:
(1) Ice Breaker/10 Minutes
(2) Relational Bible Study/40 Minutes
(3) Sign Covenant/10 Minutes (Page 42 in the Leader's Guide).

DURING THE SESSION

☐ Distribute: Give everyone a book. Collect the money.

☐ Explain: Briefly introduce the programme.

☐ Share: Tell your own reasons for wanting/ needing a spiritual "weight watchers" group.

☐ Divide: If there are more than 7, split into groups of 4. Rearrange the chairs or move into different rooms, such as the dining room, living room, etc.

☐ Regather: In the last 10 minutes, regather all groups and ask for a commitment on the Covenant — page 42. Explain the 6 disciplines, especially number 6. Sign each other's book.

AFTER THE SESSION

☐ Evaluate: Get together with the Coordinator and evaluate the session.

☐ Order: Order more books for newcomers next week. Order through bookshops or S.U. Distribution: 9-11 Clothier Road, Brislington, Bristol, BS4 5RL.

INTRODUCTION

RATIONALE: The goal for these six sessions is to become a group that really cares, like the Christian community described in Acts 2:42-47. (See pages 16-17 of the Leader's Guide.) This takes time and a common commitment to your group. (Hence, the Covenant you signed in the last session.)

The best way to explain what a Christian support community looks like is to picture a diamond. The goal is "koinonia," which is the Greek word for oneness or spiritual union.

To reach Koinonia the group needs to go around each corner of the diamond, which is another way of saying there are three stages in the process of becoming a "koinonia" depth Christian community. The first stage in this process might be called "Story Telling" . . . or telling your "God story" to each other. You shared a little about yourself in the last session. Now you need to go back and share how it all began for you . . . and where you are right now with Christ. The Relational Bible Study is designed to help you do this.

ICE BREAKER/10 Minutes

Before you move to the Bible study, take a few minutes to get up to speed with this "show and tell" exercise. Split into groups of 4 or 5 (you need not have the same people in each group as last session) and rearrange your chairs or move to different rooms if your can.

PERSONAL SCAVENGER HUNT: Take about 2 minutes in silence to go through your handbag or pockets (or clothes!) and find these four items. Then, with your group of 4, go around and "show and tell" the first item. Then, go around again on the second item, etc. Here are the items:

☐ **the most worthless thing**

☐ **the oldest thing**

☐ **the most memorable thing**

☐ **the most priceless thing**

Our Spiritual Beginnings

Goal: To share the story of your spiritual beginnings by relating your experience to the "story" of Simon Peter's "call."

RELATIONAL BIBLE STUDY
The Fisherman Who Got Hooked

Divide into groups of 4 and have someone read the Bible story aloud. Then, take 2 minutes in silence to complete the questionnaire.

To share in "Looking Into The Story" have one person share their answer to question 1, the next person question 2, etc. When you get to "My Own Story," slow down and have each person share their response to the first question. Then, go around again on the next question, etc. If you wish, you can say "I pass" on any question.

One day as Jesus was standing by the Lake of Gennesaret, with the people crowding around him and listening to the Word of God, he saw at the water's edge two boats, left there by the fishermen, who were washing their nets. He got into one of the boats, the one belonging to Simon, and asked him to put out a little from shore. Then he sat down and taught the people from the boat.

When he had finished speaking, he said to Simon, "Put out into deep water, and let down the nets for a catch."

Simon answered, "Master, we've worked hard all night and haven't caught anything. But because you say so, I will let down the nets."

When they had done so, they caught such a large number of fish that their nets began to break. So they signaled their partners in the other boat to come and help them, and they came and filled both boats so full that they began to sink.

When Simon Peter saw this, he fell at Jesus' knees and said, "Go away from me, Lord; I am a sinful man!" for he and all his companions were astonished at the catch of fish they had taken, and so were James and John, the sons of Zebedee, Simon's partners.

Then Jesus said to Simon, "Don't be afraid; from now on you will catch men." So they pulled their boats up on shore, left everything and followed him.

Luke 5:1-11 NIV

Looking into the Story

1. Do you think it was merely coincidental that Simon Peter was *"washing his nets"* when Jesus needed a boat and chose Simon's . . . or was this all part of the plan and purpose of God?
- a. merely coincidental
- b. more than coincidental
- c. a little bit of both
- d. other _____

2. If you had been Simon Peter when Jesus asked him to *"Put out into deep water, and let down the nets for a catch,"* how would you have responded?
- a. just about like Peter did
- b. wondered who this person thought he was
- c. probably made some excuse
- d. politely told Jesus to stick to his preaching
- e. suggested they try fishing tomorrow morning when there was a greater chance to catch something
- f. gone ahead with the idea but grudgingly
- g. other _____

3. When they *"caught such a large number of fish that their nets began to break,"* how do you think Simon Peter felt?
- a. ecstatic/elated/overjoyed
- b. terrible about what he said to Jesus
- c. dumbfounded

- d. aware that Jesus was everything he said he was and more
- e. completely confused
- f. other _____

4. When Simon Peter said, *"Go away from me, Lord; I am a sinful man!"* what was he really saying?
- a. "You embarrass me because you know more about fishing than I do"
- b. "I feel uncomfortable being around you because of the life I've lived"
- c. "I know you are all that you say you are, but I am not ready to follow you"
- d. "Stop bugging me. Get out of my life"
- e. "I'm not your kind of follower. I'm just a fisherman"
- f. "I'm confused. If I say 'yes,' I know that it will mean changing my lifestyle . . . and I don't think I can measure up"

5. What did it mean to Simon Peter to leave *"everything and follow Jesus"*?
- a. become a hermit
- b. leave behind his sinful ways and follow Jesus
- c. go into the Christian ministry
- d. turn over the keys of his life to Jesus and let Jesus do the driving
- e. give up his occupation
- f. start a risky "faith adventure," not knowing what the outcome would be
- g. other _____

My Own Story

1. In comparison to Simon Peter's call, my own spiritual beginning with God has been:
- a. tame
- b. more intellectual
- c. just as confusing
- d. even more crazy
- e. different, but just as real
- f. not sure
- g. other _____

2. My spiritual "boat" right now is: (choose two)
- a. sinking
- b. out for repairs
- c. stuck in the doldrums
- d. sailing at a fast clip
- e. sailing in the wrong direction
- f. afloat, but only just
- g. other _____

3. The idea of *"pushing out into the deep water"* with Jesus sounds: (choose two)
- a. scary
- b. stupid
- c. okay, but
- d. too unreal
- e. fine, if others will join me
- f. not sure what you mean
- g. just the invitation I've been waiting for
- h. other _____

4. Before I can honestly "let down my net for a catch," I need to:
- a. get myself together
- b. think it over
- c. consider the consequences
- d. straighten out a few things
- e. deal with my fear of failure
- f. clean up my life
- g. other _____

CHECKLIST FOR THE LEADER

BEFORE THE SESSION

☐ Coordinator: Spend about half of your session with the Group Leaders on their own spiritual needs, and half going over the lesson plan for this session.

☐ Group Leaders: Phone your group members. Ask them to bring a "visitor" to the next session who might be interested in joining the group. (Remember, when your group gets to 8, split into 2 groups.)

☐ Diamond: Read the fuller explanation of the "diamond" concept of group building on pages 16-17 of the Leader's Guide. Explain this concept at the beginning of the session.

☐ Agenda: Divide the time into three parts:
 (1) Rationale: Diamond concept/5 Minutes
 (2) Ice Breaker/15 Minutes
 (3) Relational Bible Study/40 minutes

DURING THE SESSION

☐ Welcome: New members. Explain the group covenant on page 42 of the Leader's Guide.

☐ Introduce: Diamond concept of group building—first stage

☐ Ice Breaker: Demonstrate the exercise by showing your 4 items, explaining a little about each item to set the pace.

☐ Divide: Split into groups of 4 before you start the group sharing.

☐ Relational Bible Study: Read the instructions and the Bible and allow 2 minutes for everyone to complete the questionnaire before starting the sharing.

☐ Empty Chair: Remind the group of the empty chair—to invite someone next week.

AFTER THE SESSION

☐ Group Leaders: Evaluate the session.

☐ Phone: Contact any absentees

☐ Order: Order more books from bookshops or S.U. Distribution: 9-11 Clothier Road, Brislington, Bristol BS4 5RL.

INTRODUCTION

RATIONALE: Telling your "story" to your Bible study group is essential for the depth-caring ministry of group members to one another, because you *understand* where a person "is coming from." In the last two sessions you shared your spiritual beginning with one another. In this session you will have the opportunity to share your "growing pains," especially where you are struggling right now in your spiritual life. The Relational Bible Study is designed for this purpose.

ICE BREAKER/10 Minutes

Before you move to the Bible study, take a few minutes to share how you *feel* about six areas in your life. Split into groups of 4 or 5 (you need not have the same people in each group as last session) and rearrange your chairs or move to different rooms in the house, such as 4 around the coffee table, 4 around the kitchen table, and 4 around the dining table.

MUSIC IN MY LIFE: Go around your small group and finish the first sentence below, "In my personal life, I'm feeling" . . . by choosing ONE of the songs: "Blues In The Night" . . . or "Feeling Groovy." Then, take the next sentence and go around again, etc. . . . until you have covered the six categories. Remember, you must choose ONE of the two songs that would best describe how you are feeling right now about that area of your life.

IN MY PERSONAL LIFE, I'M FEELING
Blues in the Night . . . . Feeling Groovy

IN MY FAMILY LIFE, I'M FEELING
Stormy Weather . . . . The Sound of Music

IN MY WORK OR CAREER, I'M FEELING
I'm Fed Up   Everything's
With This Job . . . . Coming Up Roses

IN MY SPIRITUAL LIFE, I'M FEELING
The Dead March . . Hallelujah Chorus (Messiah)

IN MY RELATIONSHIPS, I'M FEELING
Nowhere Man . . . . You Light Up My Life

AS I LOOK AT THE FUTURE, I'M FEELING
Yesterday . . . To Dream the Impossible Dream

Growing Through Difficulties

Goal: To share what you are finding difficult in your life right now and discover a way to grow through the difficulties.

RELATIONAL BIBLE STUDY
Stormy Weather
Divide into groups of 4 and have someone read the Bible story. Then, move immediately to the questions without stopping to fill out the questionnaire. Go around on the first question; then around a second time on the second question, etc.

Be sure to save 15 minutes for the questions under "My Own Story" and 5 minutes for prayer at the close.

> *That day when evening came, he said to his disciples, "Let us go over to the other side (of the lake)." Leaving the crowd behind, they took him along, just as he was, in the boat. There were also other boats with him. A furious squall (storm) came up, and the waves broke over the boat, so that it was nearly swamped. Jesus was in the stern, sleeping on a cushion. The disciples woke him and said to him, "Teacher, don't you care if we drown?"*
>
> *He got up, rebuked the wind and said to the waves, "Quiet! Be still!" Then the wind died down and it was completely calm.*
>
> *He said to his disciples, "Why are you so afraid? Do you still have no faith?"*
>
> *They were terrified and asked each other, "Who is this? Even the wind and the waves obey him!"*
>
> *Mark 4:35-41 NIV*

Looking into the Story

1. How do you think the disciples felt when Jesus, after a long day of teaching a large crowd, suggested a boat trip across the lake?
    a. frustrated
    b. relieved
    c. delighted
    d. glad to be away from people
    e. bored with the idea
    f. other _____

2. If you had been in the boat with the disciples when they ran into a storm and the boat started to fill with water, what would you have done?
    a. screamed for help
    b. taken charge of the situation
    c. started bailing water
    d. called a prayer meeting
    e. cracked jokes
    f. acted as if nothing was wrong
    g. other _____

3. Why do you think the disciples awakened Jesus?
   a. they were afraid for his safety
   b. they resented him sleeping when they needed help
   c. they remembered his teaching that very day about faith
   d. they were afraid for their own lives
   e. they wanted him to do something about the storm
   f. other _____

4. Why did Jesus allow the disciples to go through this storm?
   a. he couldn't do anything about it
   b. he didn't know there was a storm because he was sleeping
   c. he wanted to demonstrate to the disciples his power
   d. he wanted to teach the disciples a lesson in "peace"
   e. storms are just part of life
   f. other _____

My Own Story

1. My favourite way of dealing with storms in my life is: (finish the sentence)
   a. take it out on everyone else
   b. explode—like the disciples
   c. accuse God of being asleep on the job
   d. crawl into my shell
   e. try to deny that a storm exists
   f. pour out my feelings to God
   g. other _____

2. The best medicine that I have found in dealing with storms is to: (List top three)
   _____ Talk out my problems with a friend
   _____ Take a day off to be alone with God
   _____ Read a good book
   _____ Watch TV
   _____ Tackle the problem directly
   _____ Sweep it under the carpet
   _____ Take a long walk

3. The area in my life right now where there is a little "stormy weather" is: (Put a dot on the line somewhere in between "Stormy Weather" . . . and "Moonlight and Roses" for each of the situations below.)

CONCERN ABOUT MY WORK PROSPECTS

Stormy Weather _____ Moonlight and Roses

CONCERN ABOUT MY FAMILY/PARENTS/KIDS

Stormy Weather _____ Moonlight and Roses

CONCERN ABOUT MY OWN FUTURE

Stormy Weather _____ Moonlight and Roses

4. For the area above where you marked yourself closest to "Stormy Weather," how would you compare your experience here to the passage in the Bible?
   a. sensing a storm is brewing
   b. bailing water like mad to keep afloat
   c. calling out for help
   d. blaming God for being "asleep"
   e. beginning to see how God is in this
   f. other _____

5. "Quiet! Be still!" What would these words of Jesus mean in your situation above?
   a. don't worry
   b. give me time to work things out
   c. don't give up believing in God
   d. let me handle this
   e. accept the storm as a gift and learn from it
   f. "Be still and know that I am still in control"
   g. other _____

CHECKLIST FOR THE LEADER

BEFORE THE SESSION

☐ Coordinator: Split the training session between your own support needs and planning the group Bible studies.

☐ Group Leaders: Phone any absentees. Invite your group to bring a friend for the "empty chair." (Remember, you can split into smaller groups after you get to the meeting.)

☐ Research: Read Mark 4 for the background to the Bible passage. Note the teachings on faith that preceded this practical test.

☐ Agenda: Divide the time into three parts:
   (1) Ice Breaker / 15 Minutes
   (2) Relational Bible Study / 40 Minutes
   (3) Prayer / 5 Minutes

☐ Prayer: Note that prayer is introduced at the close of this session if you think the groups are ready.

DURING THE SESSION

☐ Welcome: New members. Explain the group covenant on page 42 (Leader's Guide).

☐ Rationale: Explain the need for more "story telling" (First stage).

☐ Divide: Split into groups of 4 or 5.

☐ Ice Breaker: Demonstrate by sharing your own response to the first two sentences.

☐ Relational Bible Study: Read the passage and start the sharing without waiting to fill out the questionnaire.

☐ Prayer: Give the option to each group to close in prayer, remembering any needs that have been shared.

☐ Empty Chair: Remind the group to invite anyone who needs a spiritual "weight watchers" group.

AFTER THE SESSION

☐ Evaluate: Evaluate the session

☐ Order: Order more books from bookshops or S.U. Distribution: 9-11 Clothier Road, Brislington, Bristol, BS4 5RL.

INTRODUCTION

RATIONALE: Up to this point in the course (the first 3 sessions) you have been at the first stage on the diamond—sharing your "God story" with each other. Now in this session we move to the second stage.

We call the second stage "Affirmation" or positive feedback. Instead of sharing any more about yourself, you have the opportunity to hear from the others in your Bible study group some beautiful things they have observed in your life . . . and how your "story" has been a gift to them. Pages 16-17 in the Leader's Guide has a complete explanation of the biblical basis for this kind of group feedback.

ICE BREAKER/FOUR TEMPERAMENTS

In silence read over the four temperaments below (an ancient personality test). Each temperament is described in terms of its strengths and weaknesses. Choose two temperaments that come the closest to fitting you and give yourself a percentage of each. For instance, you might see yourself as 80% Sanguine and 20% Melancholic. (Many people think themselves a mix of three or even all four; but keep it simple by concentrating on the two closest.)

SANGUINE (Super Salesman)
Strengths: Warm, friendly, outgoing, witty, optimistic, and fun to be around—the "life of the party." Good at communications, public relations, entertainment, and short bursts of energy. Basically a people person.

Weaknesses: Can be superficial, quickly discouraged, and easily hurt by rejection. Often covers up deep feelings of inferiority and inadequacy with a "happy-go-lucky" facade.

MELANCHOLIC (Super Philosopher)
Strengths: Imaginative, creative, sensitive, and artistic—a real lover of beauty, solitude, and perfection. Usually quiet, gentle, and philosophical. Able to concentrate, feel deeply, go to the heart of things, stay at something a long time, and remain calm in adversity. Basically an ideas person.

Weaknesses: Can be moody, touchy, withdrawn, and extremely shy. Easily hurt by broken relationships and capable of extreme depression. Tendency to escape from reality and relationships into themselves.

CHOLERIC (Super Leader)
Strengths: Strong, sure, self-confident, disciplined, determined, and dedicated—usually successful in whatever is undertaken. Good at organizing, taking risks, planning great endeavours, and following through with zeal. Basically a born leader.

Weaknesses: Can be cruel, sarcastic, hot tempered, and intolerant. Sometimes ruthless, unscrupulous, insensitive . . . and often "burns out" before life is over.

PHLEGMATIC (Super Friend)
Strengths: Easygoing, likable, dependable, loyal—ever cautious, conservative, and practical. A good follower, friend, and partner for a "strong-willed" person. Inclined toward unselfish service, peace-making, and the simple life. Basically a support person.

Weaknesses: Can be lazy, half-hearted, easily stepped-on and abused by the other personalities. Often deep feelings of low self-esteem and self-worth.

Session 4

Happiness Is

Goal: To affirm the strengths in each other.

RELATIONAL BIBLE STUDY
The Beatitudes
Divide into groups of 4 and follow the instructions for the Bible study. The Bible study is in three parts: (1) Self Assessment Quiz, (2) My Own Story, and (3) Affirmation.

SELF ASSESSMENT: Read over the Beatitudes and the explanation of the key word in each Beatitude. Then, circle a number between 1 and 4 to indicate how you see yourself in this area—1 being very weak . . . and 4 being very strong.

"Blessed are the poor in Spirit,
for theirs is the kingdom of heaven.
Blessed are those who mourn,
for they will be comforted.
Blessed are the meek,
for they will inherit the earth.
Blessed are those who hunger and thirst
for righteousness,
for they will be filled.

Blessed are the merciful,
for they will be shown mercy.
Blessed are the pure in heart,
for they will see God.
Blessed are the peacemakers,
for they will be called sons of God.
Blessed are those who are persecuted
because of righteousness,
for theirs is the kingdom of heaven."

Matthew 5:3-10 NIV

The Beatitudes, with which Jesus begins his Sermon on the Mount, describe the character of those who are spiritually "blessed" or "happy." The Good News Bible starts each one with the word "happy," as in the Self-Assessment Quiz.

Happy are those who know they are SPIRITUALLY POOR.
Have you come to the place where you can admit to others that you don't have all the answers? That you have needs? That you need God and others? Are you able to let others know where you are "spiritually poor"?

1   2   3   4

Happy are those who MOURN.
Are you able to show your emotions? To express your feelings? To feel deeply your own and others' needs? Do you give others permission to show their emotions?

1   2   3   4

Happy are those who are HUMBLE.
Are you the kind of person that enables other people to come forward because of your gentle spirit? Are you able to lead from behind, by holding yourself back?

1   2   3   4

Happy are those whose GREATEST DESIRE is to do what God requires.
Are you as excited about God's leading in the daily decisions of your life as you ought to be? What really motivates you? In the hard-nosed decisions of your professional life, where does God come in? Do you really put people above things?

1   2   3   4

Happy are those who are MERCIFUL to others.
Are you a "caring" kind of person? Sensitive to others' needs? Giving yourself without thought of return?

1 2 3 4

_____

Happy are the PURE IN HEART.
Have you come to terms with yourself to the extent that you are able to be yourself? The same person in church that you are in the world? The same language? Are you transparent? Open? Honest? Willing to let others know you deeply?

1 2 3 4

_____

Happy are those who work for PEACE.
Are you able to reconcile differences without destroying their uniqueness? Is your own manner disarming? Do you bring people together? Can you accept genuinely and sincerely those who do not agree with you?

1 2 3 4

_____

Happy are those who are PERSECUTED because they do what God requires.
Are you able to take criticism from those nearest to you without reacting defensively? How about from your children? Do personal attacks tend to destroy your own self-image?

1 2 3 4

_____

My Own Story: Think over your outlook on life in light of the Sermon on the Mount / Beatitudes.

1. I see the attitude toward life that Jesus lived and spoke about as: (circle one in each category)

Basic to the Christian life	**The ideal for the Christian life**
Something I aspire to	**Something I have given up on**
The doorway to happiness	**A dead-end street**
The basis for life in community	**The basis for a future kingdom**

2. When I compare my own mental attitude to the attitudes Jesus described in the Scripture, I feel like: (circle one)

a. **giving up**
b. **trying harder**
c. **applying for an overhaul**
d. **starting all over again**

e. **something is wrong**
f. **rethinking my scale of values**
g. **ask me tomorrow**
h. **other** _____

AFFIRMATION: Now, go back over the Beatitudes and think of the others in your sharing group . . . in SILENCE. Jot down his or her name on the line next to the Beatitude where you see each person is strongest.

For example, you might jot down Mary's name next to MOURN because you have observed Mary as a very "feeling" person . . . and you might put Tom's name next to HUMBLE because you see Tom as a very gentle person, etc.

HOW TO SHARE: Here is how to share the three parts of this questionnaire. On SELF ASSESSMENT, ask each person to share only TWO areas: (a) where you marked yourself the _strongest_ and (b) where you marked yourself the _weakest_.

☐ On MY OWN STORY, briefly describe how you answered each question.

☐ On AFFIRMATION, ask one person in your group to sit in silence while the others explain where they jotted down this person's name and why. Then, ask the next person to sit in silence while the others "affirm" this person, etc.

CHECKLIST FOR THE LEADER

BEFORE THE SESSION

☐ Coordinator: Split the training session for Group Leaders between support for each other and going over the agenda.

☐ Group Leaders: Phone your group and ask them to invite a friend to the group this week. Check up on any needs they shared last week.

☐ Agenda: Divide the time into three parts:
(1) Ice Breaker / 15 minutes
(2) Relational Bible Study / 40 Minutes
(3) Prayer / 5 Minutes

☐ Relational Bible Study: Note the final sharing process where one person in a group sits in silence while the others share the strength they have observed in this person's life. Practise this in your team meeting.

DURING THE SESSION

☐ Welcome: New members. Explain the covenant on page 42 (Leader's Guide).

☐ Rationale: Explain the diamond—second stage—affirmation.

☐ Ice Breaker: Demonstrate this by explaining the two predominant temperaments you see in yourself before asking the groups to share.

☐ Relational Bible Study: In the last stage of sharing—Affirmation—explain carefully how one person sits in silence while the others in the group share the strength they see in this person.

☐ Prayer: Close in prayer in each group.

☐ Empty Chair: Remind the group to invite others.

AFTER THE SESSION

☐ Evaluate: Evaluate the session.

☐ Plan Ahead: Consider how to follow this course—perhaps with one of the other books in the Serendipity series.

☐ Order: Order more books from bookshops or S.U. Distribution: 9-11 Clothier Road, Brislington, Bristol, BS4 5RL.Telephone (0272) 719107.

INTRODUCTION

RATIONALE: In this session, you will move on to the third stage in the diamond concept in "becoming a Christian community." The third stage is called "Goal Setting," which is another way of saying that you move into sharing where you think God wants you to stretch, grow, and move on in your spiritual journey.

Sharing these NEEDS with one another is scary, risky, and demands a lot from the group in the way of support, encouragement, prayer and "body ministry." This is the reason why we carefully structure the first few sessions of a group—to keep you from going too far until the group is ready to support you in your needs. (More is said about the biblical concept of "body ministry" on page 17 of the Leader's Guide.)

ICE BREAKER/STRESS TEST

This is the test that Dr. Richard Rahe developed for measuring stress. If you score more than 150 points on this test in the last six months, you are probably under a lot of stress right now. After you have figured out your score, get together in groups of 4. What do you need to do about them?

EVENT	STRESS POINTS
Death of spouse	100
Divorce	73
Marital separation	65
Jail term	63
Death of close family member	63
Personal injury or illness	53
Marriage	50
Loss of job	47
Marital reconciliation	45
Retirement	45
Health problem of family member	44
Pregnancy	40
Sex difficulties	39
Gain of new family member	39
Business readjustment	39
Change in financial state	38
Death of a close friend	37
Change in line of work	36
Increased arguments with spouse	35
Large mortgage taken out	31
Foreclosure of mortgage or loan	30
Change in work responsibilities	29
Son or daughter leaving home	29
Trouble with in-laws	29
Major personal achievement	28
Wife starting or stopping work	26
Starting or leaving school/college	26
Change in living conditions	25
Revision of personal habits	24
Trouble with boss	23
Change in work hours	20
Change in residence	20
Change in school/college	20
Change in recreation	19
Change in church activities	19
Change in social activities	18
Small mortgage taken out	17
Change in sleeping habits	16
Change in family get-togethers	15
Change in eating habits	15
Holiday	13
Christmas	12
Minor violation of the law	11
TOTAL	_____

Asking and Receiving

Goal: To share with one another where you need to stretch, grow, and move on in your spiritual journey; and apply Jesus' teaching on prayer to it.

RELATIONAL BIBLE STUDY
Three Parables on Prayer

Divide into groups of 4 and read the first Bible passage. Let one person respond to the first question, the next person respond to the second question, etc. Then, read the second passage and rotate on the questions again. Finally, read the third passage and rotate around on the last questions.

When you get to the Application, slow down and let each person explain the two things where they need help. Save time at the end for prayer.

One day Jesus was praying in a certain place. When he finished, one of his disciples said to him, "Lord, teach us to pray, just as John taught his disciples."

He said to them, "When you pray, say:

" 'Father,
hallowed be your name,
your kingdom come.
Give us each day our daily bread.
Forgive us our sins,
*   for we also forgive everyone who sins against us.*
And lead us not into temptation.' "

Then he said to them, "Suppose one of you has a friend, and he goes to him at midnight and says, 'Friend, lend me three loaves of bread, because a friend of mine on a journey has come to me, and I have nothing to set before him.'

"Then the one inside answers, 'Don't bother me. The door is already locked, and my children are with me in bed. I can't get up and give you anything.' I tell you, though he will not get up and give him the bread because he is his friend, yet because of the man's persistence he will get up and give him as much as he needs.

"So I say to you: Ask and it will be given to you; seek and you will find; knock and the door will be opened to you. For everyone who asks receives; he who seeks finds; and to him who knocks, the door will be opened.

Luke 11:1-10 NIV

1. If my neighbour rang me up at 3 a.m. asking for bread, I would probably: (circle one)

  a. say, "You've got the wrong number"
  b. listen, but say "Phone me in the morning"
  c. get up and bake some bread
  d. consider who it was before I decided to help
  e. get out of bed and get something to shut him up
  f. (expletive deleted)
  g. other _____

2. The point of this parable is that: (As a group, discuss the possibilities)

  a. we give up too soon when we ask God for things
  b. we should refuse to take "no" for an answer
  c. God is as responsive as our reluctant neighbour
  d. God gives us what we want, not in exasperation, but in joy
  e. we should keep praying, no matter what the answer seems to be
  f. (a combination of two or three)

(Move on to the end of this parable before you try to arrive at a final conclusion)

> *"Which of you fathers, if your son asks for a fish, will give him a snake instead? Or if he asks for an egg, will give him a scorpion? If you then, though you are evil, know how to give good gifts to your children, how much more will your Father in heaven give the Holy Spirit to those who ask him!"*
>
> Luke 11:11-13 NIV

3. In this second parable, what is the point that Jesus is making? (Circle all that apply)

a. Father knows best

b. Human fathers seek the best for their kids

c. God will not withhold any good thing from one of his children

d. If we don't receive what we ask for, it must be because God knew better

e. God always answers prayer, but not always in the way we expect

4. In light of these two parables, what does God want to give us more than anything? (Circle all that apply)

a. All the bread, fish and eggs we can eat

b. Whatever we ask, in all cases

c. Whatever we need, but He decides

d. The Holy Spirit, if we ask

e. Other _____

> *Then Jesus told his disciples a parable to show them that they should always pray and not give up. He said: "In a certain town there was a judge who neither feared God nor cared about men. And there was a widow in that town who kept coming to him with the plea, 'Grant me justice against my adversary.'*
>
> *"For some time he refused. But finally he said to himself, 'Even though I don't fear God or care about men, yet because this widow keeps bothering me, I will see that she gets justice, so that she won't eventually wear me out with her coming!' "*
>
> *And the Lord said, "Listen to what the unjust judge says. And will not God bring about justice for his chosen ones, who cry out to him day and night? Will he keep putting them off? I tell you, he will see that they get justice, and quickly."*
>
> Luke 18:1-8 NIV

5. How is the judge in this parable like the neighbour in the first parable?

6. What is the point of this parable? (Circle any that apply)

a. God is like the judge; if we pester Him long enough, He will answer us

b. God is not like the judge; He responds speedily to our requests

c. We ought to pray without ceasing, expecting God to answer

d. Other _____

7. This passage emphasizes that God is: (circle any that apply)

a. a God of justice

b. easily bothered by trivial prayer requests

c. wise and righteous

d. punctual and responsive

e. other _____

APPLICATION: Meditate for a moment on the passage below. Then, jot down one or two things that cause you some concern that you would like to hand over to God in prayer. Then, use these items as the basis for a time of prayer in your group.

> *Do not be anxious about anything, but in everything, by prayer and petition, with thanksgiving, present your requests to God. And the peace of God, which transcends all understanding, will guard your hearts and your minds in Christ Jesus.*
>
> Philippians 4:6-7 NIV

The two things I want to turn over to God in prayer right now are:

CHECKLIST FOR THE LEADER

BEFORE THE SESSION

☐ Coordinator: Continue training your group leaders. Discuss how to follow this course—perhaps with one of the other books in this Serendipity series.

☐ Group Leaders: Phone your group. Ask them to invite a friend. Check up on any needs that were shared.

☐ Agenda: Divide the time into three parts:
(1) Ice Breaker / 10 Minutes
(2) Relational Bible Study / 40 Minutes
(3) Prayer / 10 Minutes

☐ Relational Bible Study: Note the different approach in sharing. There are three Bible passages and you rotate answering the questions unless the question asks for a group consensus.

DURING THE SESSION

☐ Welcome: New members. Explain the covenant on page 42 (Leader's Guide).

☐ Rationale: Explain the diamond — third stage — including the biblical principles on page 17 of the Leader's Guide.

☐ Ice Breaker: Don't spend a lot of time here.

☐ Relational Bible Study: Skim the questions until the last question under each Bible passage.

☐ Prayer: Save plenty of time for each person to share their Application and pray for each other!

☐ Empty Chair: Remind the group to invite friends.

AFTER THE SESSION

☐ Decide: Decide what you are going to do after this course.

☐ Order: Order more books from bookshops or S.U. Distribution: 9-11 Clothier Road, Brislington, Bristol, BS4 5RL. **Telephone (0272) 71907.**

(Our thanks to the Menlo Park Presbyterian Church, Menlo Park, California, for this Bible study.)

INTRODUCTION

RATIONALE: With this session, you complete the diamond of "group building."

☐ First Stage/Story Telling: Sharing your "God-story" with each other—your spiritual beginning, journey, struggles, significant people, places, and events.

☐ Second Stage/Affirmation: Responding to each other's story with positive feedback—the strengths, gifts, and the things you appreciate in each other.

☐ Third Stage/Goal Setting: Sharing again (this time on a deeper level) where you are stretching, struggling, and hurting right now—and where you need support, encouragement, and healing.

Now we come to the ultimate goal of any sharing group—koinonia, or depth support community. The Apostle Paul speaks of this experience as the "body of Christ"—various members with different spiritual gifts—that "build up" one another in love . . . until the whole "body . . . becomes mature, attaining to the whole measure of the fullness of Christ." Ephesians 4:11-13.

ICE BREAKER/10 Minutes

Before you move to the Bible study, take a few minutes to share some of the insights you have discovered about each other during this course.

I PREDICT: Jot down the names of the people in your group next to the thing each person might be famous for (or at least best qualified for). Then, ask one person to sit in silence while the others share where they put this person's name and why. Then, move to the next person and repeat the process, etc.

____ **be the first woman to win the Grand National**
____ **run a pirate video operation**
____ **rise to the top in the diplomatic service**
____ **be a world famous hairdresser**
____ **get arrested for streaking on a First Division football pitch**
____ **write an advice column for the love-lorn**
____ **become a campaigner for proportional representation**
____ **become an underworld detective**
____ **advertise ladies underwear on T.V.**
____ **make a fortune in privatised public conveniences**
____ **write a best-selling novel about your love life**
____ **replace Paul Daniels on That's Magic**
____ **win the pools**

Becoming a Group that Cares

Goal: To complete the diamond process in becoming a group that cares by comparing your experiences together with the pattern Jesus set for his followers.

RELATIONAL BIBLE STUDY
The Jesus Pattern

Divide into groups of 4 and work as a group through the questions after you read the Bible passage. Go around on the first question. Then, go around on the second question, etc.

Save at least 15 minutes at the close for the APPLICATION/CHILDREN'S ZOO sharing exercise.

> *It was just before the Passover Feast. Jesus knew that the time had come for him to leave this world and go to the Father. Having loved his own who were in the world, he now showed them the full extent of his love.*
>
> *The evening meal was being served, and the devil had already prompted Judas Iscariot, son of Simon, to betray Jesus. Jesus knew that the Father had put all things under his power, and that he had come from God and was returning to God; so he got up from the meal, took off his outer clothing, and wrapped a towel around his waist. After that, he poured water into a basin and began to wash his disciples' feet, drying them with the towel that was wrapped around him. . . .*
>
> *When he had finished washing their feet, he put on his clothes and returned to his place. "Do you understand what I have done for you?" he asked them. "You call me 'Teacher' and 'Lord,' and rightly so, for that is what I am. Now that I, your Lord and Teacher, have washed your feet, you also should wash one another's feet. I have set you an example that you should do as I have done for you."*
>
> *John 13:1-5, 12-15 NIV*

1. If I had been one of the disciples when Jesus came to wash their feet, I would have: (choose one)
 a. felt humiliated
 b. refused
 c. felt like refusing
 d. insisted on washing his feet instead
 e. felt bad/guilty about my attitude
 f. considered it the greatest honour
 g. other _____

2. In my estimation, the reason why Jesus washed the feet of his disciples was to: (choose the closest)
 a. shame them for their unwillingness to wash each other's feet
 b. share his genuine love for them on their last night together
 c. teach them a lesson in servanthood
 d. demonstrate what a leader really is
 e. other _____

3. The reason why we do not see more spiritual "footwashing" among Christians today is because we:
   a. don't need each other
   b. don't know we need each other
   c. don't know each other's deeper needs
   d. don't want to know each other's needs
   e. don't want others to know our deeper needs

4. Since being in this Bible study group, my greatest growth has been in the area of my: (list top 2)
   ____ personal discipline
   ____ Bible understanding
   ____ willingness to share myself
   ____ commitment to Christ
   ____ relationships with others
   ____ concern for others

5. Right now, if Jesus were to "wash my feet" (knowing my need as he does), Jesus would probably:
   a. put his arms around me and give me a great big hug
   b. take a long time just being with me
   c. give me a big kick in the pants
   d. tell me how proud he was of me
   e. wash my feet just like he did the disciples
   f. pass on without saying a word
   g. other _____

6. Right now, I feel that I am living up to:
   a. all that I know is God's will for my life
   b. all that I am willing to know of God's will for my life
   c. less than what I know is God's will for my life
   d. just what's possible—I can't do any more
   e. what I want to do. Please don't bother me with God's will.
   f. other _____

APPLICATION: Take a moment and look over the list of animals in this Children's Zoo. Choose the animal that reveals something about what has happened to you since being in this group. Then, go around your group and let each person explain the animal they identify with and why.

_____ **CUDDLY BOA CONSTRICTOR: Because I would like to wrap up this whole group and take you home with me.**

_____ **PLAYFUL PORPOISE: Because you have helped me to find a new freedom and a whole new world to play in.**

_____ **COLOURFUL PEACOCK: Because you have told me that I am beautiful, and I have started to believe it, and it is changing my life.**

_____ **SAFARI ELEPHANT: Because you have helped me enjoy this new adventure and I am not going to forget it . . . or this group. Can hardly wait for the next safari.**

_____ **LOVABLE HIPPOPOTAMUS: Because you have let me surface and bask in the warm sunshine of God's love.**

_____ **LYNX EYED LEOPARD: Because you have helped me to look very closely at myself and see some of the spots . . . and you have told me it's OK to be this way.**

_____ **DANCING BEAR: Because you have taught me to dance in the midst of pain, and you have helped me to reach out and hug again.**

_____ **ROARING LION: Because you have let me get down off my perch and roll in the grass, and not even worry about my mane.**

_____ **WILD EAGLE: Because you have helped to heal my wings, and taught me how to soar again.**

_____ **TOWERING GIRAFFE: Because you have helped me to hold my head up and stick my neck out, and reach over the fences I have built.**

_____ **ALL-WEATHER DUCK: Because you have taught me to enjoy the weather (even on rainy days) and to celebrate the hard times like a duck in a storm.**

_____ **OSTRICH IN LOVE: Because you have loved me so much that I have taken my head out of the sand, and found a whole new reason for living.**

CHECKLIST FOR THE LEADER

BEFORE THE SESSION

☐ Coordinator: Continue your support meeting for Group Leaders. You will have to decide about how to handle the next phase—either let each group decide or make the decision for all groups.

☐ Overview: This being the last session in this course, the Relational Bible Study and Application has been designed to give time for personal evaluation at the close. Explain background for Bible passage—the Last Supper, the last night before Christ's death.

☐ Agenda: Three parts to the session:
   (1) Ice Breaker / 10 Minutes
   (2) Relational Bible Study / 30 Minutes
   (3) Application / 20 Minutes

☐ Decision: The group will have to make a decision to disband, do another Serendipity course, or move to another kind of programme.

DURING THE SESSION

☐ Welcome: New members.

☐ Rationale: Go over the diamond concept—Koinonia.

☐ Ice Breaker: Don't spend more than 10 minutes.

☐ Relational Bible Study: The emphasis is on group and personal evaluation. Be sure to save at least 20 minutes for the Application.

☐ Decision: What to do as a group.

AFTER THE SESSION:

☐ Evaluate: Evaluate your decision with the Coordinator for all groups.

☐ Order: Order more books from bookshops or S.U. Distribution: 9-11 Clothier Road, Brislington, Bristol, BS4 5RL. Telephone (0272) 71907.

I Believe

BOOK TWO

6 SESSIONS TO EXAMINE WHAT YOU BELIEVE

This is one of two courses used for introducing small groups to Serendipity. Choose one or both. Before you start on this course, make sure that everyone in the group is committed to the covenant on the next page.

WHY RENEW THE COVENANT?

Before you start on this unit, it is important to recall the covenant you made together.

In this unit, the purpose is slightly different—to examine what you believe. But the disciplines are the same. At the first session, you need to go over these disciplines and sign the covenant again—reaffirming your commitment.

1. Attendance: Priority is given to the group meetings. Except in case of emergency, you promise to be present on time.

2. Participation: The purpose of this unit is to examine what you believe—using the Apostles Creed as a foundation. You are willing to share the stories of your spiritual journey, including the struggles, the joys, and the pain.

3. Confidentiality: Anything that is shared in the group is kept in strict confidence. This is not a therapy group, but information will be shared from time to time that should not be repeated outside the group.

4. Accountability: At the close of every session, an opportunity is given for you to share new goals you want to set for your life. When you set a goal and ask the others in the group to support you in these goals, you are giving permission to the group "to hold you accountable."

5. Accessibility: The group is for people who recognise their own weaknesses and acknowledge the need of help from others to overcome temptation, spiritual depression, and continuing weakness. In asking to be in a group, you are admitting you need support . . . and that you are willing to support others in the same condition.

6. Evangelisation: The group is willing and ready at any time to adopt new people who need the support of your group. In forming a group you agree to "keep an empty chair" for anyone who wants to join your group and is willing to agree to share its disciplines.

GROUP COVENANT

For the next 6 weeks, we agree to the following disciplines as a group.

☐ Attendance: To give priority to the group meetings.

☐ Participation: To give ourselves to the group — to examine what we believe and to share our spiritual journeys with each other.

☐ Confidentiality: To keep anything that is shared strictly confidential.

☐ Accountability: To give permission to group members to hold you accountable for goals *you* set for *yourself*.

☐ Accessibility: To give each other the right to call upon one another in times of temptation and need—even in the middle of the night.

☐ Evangelisation: To keep the door open to others in our church who need encouragement.

SPECIFICS:

We will meet on _____ (day of week).

We will meet at _____ (home/place).

The meeting will begin at _____ and close at _____.

ORGANISATION: What do we want to do about . . .

☐ Refreshments: _____

☐ Baby-sitting: _____

☐ Newcomers: _____

☐ Absence: _____

I will try with God's help to be a regular, faithful, caring member of this group.

Signed: _____

NAMES OF GROUP MEMBERS	PHONE

As new people join the group, add their names to this list.

I BELIEVE: A GUIDE TO THE COURSE

1 God

RELATIONAL BIBLE STUDY
Holy Smoke
God used a burning bush to get the attention of Moses and to remind Moses of who He was. What concept did you have of God when you were between 7 and 12? What is your concept of God now? How would you compare your concept of God with the God who was revealed to Moses? Here is an opportunity to share how your concept of God has developed since you were a child, and how you see God now.

DEEPER BIBLE STUDY
The Attributes of God
Can you connect your concept of God with your view of yourself? Have you applied the characteristics of God to the implications for your own life? For instance, if God is ALL POWERFUL, what difference does this make to the way you think? Here is an opportunity for you to put things together and see if you are appropriating all that is yours as a child of God.

2 Jesus Christ

RELATIONAL BIBLE STUDY
Who Am I?
If you stopped the average person in the street and asked, "Who is Jesus Christ?" what would their answer be? Here is an opportunity to compare the image the "man in the street" has about Jesus with your own, and to deal with the issue of discipleship when Jesus said, "If anyone would come after me he must deny himself, take up his cross and follow me."

DEEPER BIBLE STUDY
St. Paul on Jesus
The Apostle Paul describes Jesus Christ with 10 statements in his letter to the Christians at Colossae. Take this list and see what difference it makes in your own life. For instance, the first statement is: "Christ is the image of the invisible God." If this is true, is it also true that to know Jesus Christ is to know God because Jesus is the exact likeness of God? These 10 conclusions about yourself are for you to decide.

3 Holy Spirit

RELATIONAL BIBLE STUDY
Famous Last Words
According to John's Gospel, on the night before his death Jesus taught his disciples about the Holy Spirit. Imagine you are there with the disciples and try to understand the promise of the Spirit in terms of the actual situation in which it was given. Then, compare this promise to how much of the Holy Spirit you appropriate in your own everyday life.

DEEPER BIBLE STUDY
The Fruit of the Spirit
Take a look at yourself and measure how much the "fruit of the Spirit" is ripening in your own spiritual life. Then ask one person in your group to sit in silence while the others affirm the fruit you have observed in each other's lives. Here is an opportunity to point out the good things you have observed in and about one another.

4 The Church Universal

RELATIONAL BIBLE STUDY
Life Together
Acts 2:42-47 describes the early church soon after Pentecost. Look at your own church and Bible study group in light of the six characteristics of the early church:
(a) Study of the Apostles' teaching, (b) Miracles, (c) Caring, (d) Worship together, (e) House groups, and (f) Growth. Could this model work today?

DEEPER BIBLE STUDY
Body Building
The Apostle Paul follows up his challenge to "find the will of God" with a description of seven "spiritual gifts." Look over these seven gifts, and as you understand yourself, decide which gifts you feel are yours. This may help you to understand the "will of God" for you . . . and your particular place and ministry within the "Body of Christ."

5 The Forgiveness of Sins

RELATIONAL BIBLE STUDY
Pharisee or Tax Collector
In the parable of the Pharisee and the Tax Collector, to which person would you feel closest? Which of your own problems would you share with the Pharisee? And which with the Tax Collector? Use this challenging parable to re-examine the meaning of sin, and why the "Tax Collector went home justified (forgiven)."

DEEPER BIBLE STUDY
All This and Heaven Too
Look at some of the statements that Jesus makes about you as a believer — such as, "You are a new creation . . . reconciled . . . justified . . . chosen . . . adopted . . . redeemed . . . a citizen of heaven . . . and a very special person." After each statement (and the Scripture to back it up), put a dot on the line — somewhere between NO and YES to indicate your response to this fact.

6 Resurrection and Life

RELATIONAL BIBLE STUDY
Doubting Thomas
Before you jump on Thomas for doubting the second-hand report that Jesus was alive, look at your own spiritual journey and share some of the questions you have had and the evidence you expect God to give you. In times of doubt what has helped you most? This last session should be an encouraging experience.

DEEPER BIBLE STUDY
Pick a Promise to Grow On
Look ahead a bit and choose one of the promises in the list as a verse for your life . . . choose another for the next step in your spiritual journey. Look back on the course and affirm the people who have shared their life with you during this course.

INTRODUCTION

The next six sessions in your group will be based on the Apostles Creed—an early confession of faith in the Christian church. The early Christians were being misled by false teaching. They needed a statement that summarised what was unique about the Christian faith. This is what they came up with.

I believe in God, the Father Almighty

This session will be spent dealing with the first sentence in the Apostles Creed—about God.

In the Old Testament, there are two basic words for God. ELOHIM and YAHWEH. The word ELOHIM is used when speaking of the *power* and *might* of God—the infinite and eternal being that created the universe and rules over it.

In the Apostles Creed, the meaning of ELOHIM is brought out by the addition "God . . . Almighty"; that is, I believe in the One supreme ruler of the universe, who created, sustains, preserves and upholds the universe by his power.

The second word for God in the Old Testament brings out a completely different side of God's character. It was the name given to Moses when Moses asked God for the "name" I am to tell the people when they ask me "Who shall I say sent me?" God replied, "Tell them YAHWEH sent you."

This is the very, very personal name for God that refers to his *personal* relationship with the Hebrews as their deliverer, redeemer and Saviour.

ICE BREAKER/Optional

Here's a simple "conversation starter" to set the stage for this session. Take 2 minutes in silence to complete the exercise. Then, share in 4's.

CONCEPTS OF GOD: Below are a series of ideas about God. Put a "7" beside the idea of God you had at age seven; a "12" beside the idea of God you had at age twelve, and an "N" for now.

____ The all-powerful creator of the universe
____ The giver of grace and forgiveness
____ The architect of the harmony/beauty in the universe
____ A friend that I can confide in
____ The source of life who breathed "new life" into me
____ The suffering servant who washed feet and died to save the world
____ The teacher of a peaceful, simple life
____ The "Lamb of God" given as a sacrifice for sin
____ The judge that sends people to hell
____ The "father" waiting for the prodigal to return
____ The person the Christmas story is about

Session 1

God, the Father Almighty

Goal: To examine what you believe about God, the Father.

Option 1
RELATIONAL BIBLE STUDY
Holy Smoke

After the Scripture passage has been read, get together with one person from your group and work together on the questions under "Looking Into the Story." Then, continue on your own on the questions under "My Own Story."

> *Now Moses was tending the flock of Jethro his father-in-law, the priest of Midian, and he led the flock to the far side of the desert and came to Horeb, the mountain of God. There the angel of the Lord appeared to him in flames of fire from within a bush. Moses saw that though the bush was on fire it did not burn up. So Moses thought, "I will go over and see this strange sight—why the bush does not burn up."*
>
> *When the Lord saw that he had gone over to look, God called to him from within the bush, "Moses, Moses!"*
>
> *And Moses said, "Here I am."*
>
> *"Do not come any closer," God said. "Take off your sandals, for the place where you are standing is holy ground." Then he said, "I am the God of your father, the God of Abraham, the God of Isaac and the God of Jacob." At this, Moses hid his face, because he was afraid to look at God.*
>
> Exodus 3:1-6, NIV

Looking Into the Story:

1. If you had been Moses in this situation, what would you have done? (choose two)
a. gone back to bed
b. wonder what's happening
c. given up late night films
d. what Moses did
e. hollered for help

2. Why did God appear to Moses in this particular way?
a. Moses was trying to get away from God
b. Moses needed a challenge
c. God needed to get his attention
d. Moses needed to be reminded of who God was
e. God wanted the relationship to begin unforgettably

3. What is the image of God that comes over to you in this passage? (Place in order 1-3 after finishing this sentence: "God is . . . .")
____ all powerful
____ not to be treated lightly
____ far away
____ mysterious
____ everywhere
____ supernatural
____ awesome
____ holy
____ compassionate
____ personal
____ sovereign over everything
____ a keeper of promises
____ the Creator of all things
____ the Ruler of the universe
____ speaking to anyone who will listen
____ wanting to show concern for all

My Own Story:

1. In comparison to Moses' story, my own meetings with God have been: *(Choose two.)*
   a. just as exciting
   b. more personal
   c. rather tame
   d. just as life-changing
   e. more intellectual
   f. different, but just as real

2. If I had to compare my experience of God to nature, it would be like:
   a. a sunrise—gradual
   b. a bolt of lightning—electrifying
   c. a breathtaking view
   d. deep mysterious ocean
   e. quiet, intimate garden
   f. the spectacular mountains (with valleys)

Option 2
DEEPER BIBLE STUDY
The Attributes of God

Here are 7 characteristics of God. Read the definition and the Scripture. Then, respond to the statement below by ticking ☐ YES, ☐ NO or ☐ MAYBE

1. ALL POWERFUL: God can do anything. God is limited only by the limits he sets upon himself.
"Ah, Sovereign Lord, you have made the heavens and the earth by your great power and outstretched arm. Nothing is too hard for you." Jeremiah 32:17, NIV
If God is all powerful, I can do all things through his power. ☐ YES ☐ NO ☐ MAYBE

2. GLORIOUS: The beauty and splendor in the universe are reflections of the glory of the Creator.
"The heavens declare the glory of God; the skies proclaim the work of his hands." Psalm 19:1
If I am a part of God's beautiful creation, I must be a valuable person.
☐ YES ☐ NO ☐ MAYBE

3. EVER PRESENT: God is present everywhere.
"Where can I go from your Spirit? Where can I flee from your presence? If I go up to the heavens, you are there; if I make my bed in the depths, you are there. If I rise on the wings of the dawn, if I settle on the far side of the sea; even there your hand will guide me, your right hand will hold me fast." Psalm 139:7-10, NIV
If God is everywhere, I cannot hide from God. ☐ YES ☐ NO ☐ MAYBE

4. SOVEREIGN: God is the ruler of the universe—in complete control.
"Be still, and know that I am God; I will be exalted among the nations, I will be exalted in the earth." Psalm 46:10, NIV
If God is in control, I don't have to worry about a thing. ☐ YES ☐ NO ☐ MAYBE

5. HOLY: God is absolute purity, righteousness, and holiness (the opposite of sin).
"This is the message we have heard from him and declare to you: God is light; in him there is no darkness at all." 1 John 1:5, NIV
If God is holy, those who have fellowship with God must be holy too . . . including me.
☐ YES ☐ NO ☐ MAYBE

6. JUST: God is the moral judge of the universe; he judges fairly and has provided a just way to forgive sinners.
"God presented him [Christ] as a sacrifice of atonement. . . . He did this to demonstrate his justice . . . he did it to demonstrate his justice at the present time, so as to be just and the one who justifies the man who has faith in Jesus." Romans 3:25-26, NIV
If God is just, he must punish sin, and condemn to death those who sin.
☐ YES ☐ NO ☐ MAYBE

7. LOVE: God is absolute love. To satisfy his justice, he provided the payment for sin in the death of his Son, Jesus Christ, the "lamb of God."
"For God so loved the world that he gave his one and only Son, that whoever believes in him shall not perish but have eternal life." John 3:16, NIV
God offers me a complete pardon for sin through the sacrifice of Jesus Christ as the "lamb of God" in my place. ☐ YES ☐ NO ☐ MAYBE

APPLICATION: Put a dot on the line—somewhere in between the two extremes—to indicate how you are feeling.

This study of the attributes of God make me feel . . .
Worth nothing _____ Worth everything

Which attribute of God means the most to you right now? _____

CHECKLIST FOR THE LEADER
BEFORE THE SESSION

☐ Coordinator: Call together all group leaders to plan/discuss any problems. Review pages 5-7 and 16-17 of the Leader's Guide.

☐ Group Leaders: Note the options in this lesson plan: an Ice Breaker and two different Bible studies. The Deeper Bible Study is more demanding.

☐ Covenant: Even though you have signed the Covenant in the first unit, take time to review and sign the Covenant again for this unit.

☐ Apostles Creed: Do some research on this creed. The Introduction and Ice Breaker in the special box will help you.

DURING THE SESSION

☐ Welcome: Welcome new members. Explain the "weight watcher" group concept, and the disciplines in the Covenant.

☐ Divide: Split into groups of 4. Rearrange the chairs, like 4 around the dining table, 4 around the coffee table, etc.

☐ Ice Breaker: The ice breaker at the bottom of the Introduction box is a good way to start the sharing.

☐ Optional Bible Studies: Choose between the two options. The Relational Bible Study is easier to share because of the multiple choice questions.

☐ Covenant: Sign the covenant again.

☐ Empty Chair: Remind the group to invite someone next week.

AFTER THE SESSION

☐ Group Leaders: Evaluate the session with the Coordinator.

☐ Phone: Phone your group members. Remind them of the empty chair.

☐ Order: Order more books for newcomers from bookshops or S.U. Distribution: 9-11 Clothier Road, Brislington, Bristol BS4 5RL. Telephone (0272) 71907.

INTRODUCTION

The second statement in the Apostles Creed concerns Jesus Christ:

> "I believe in Jesus Christ his only Son our Lord. He was conceived by the power of the Holy Spirit and born of the Virgin Mary. He suffered under Pontius Pilate, was crucified, died and was buried. . . . On the third day he rose again. He ascended into heaven, and is seated at the right hand of the Father. He will come again to judge the living and the dead."

This brief summary of facts concerning Jesus Christ is a direct refutation of the false teaching concerning Jesus given by the Gnostics.

The Gnostic teaching was that God was nameless and unknowable—a remote Divine Being. At the other end of the spectrum is the material universe—the dumping ground of all evil. Between these two extremes is a series of "emanations" or stairs by which man can work his way toward God by divesting himself of the evil world. This teaching led to all sorts of attempts to deny our humanity—like some of the cults of today demonstrate.

I believe in Jesus Christ

When it came to Jesus Christ, the Gnostics had to do something to keep the Divine spiritual nature from getting contaminated with the material, evil universe. They accomplished this by denying that Christ was actually "incarnated" in human flesh. Instead, they taught that Christ (the Divine nature) entered Jesus (the human being) at the baptism and left the human being at the moment of the crucifixion. Thus, Jesus Christ was neither born as a man nor suffered as a man. Christ (the Divine nature) simply used the human body of Jesus as a phantom body.

Against this false teaching, the Apostles Creed affirms the basics of the gospel: □ The incarnation—God coming to live in human flesh. □ The virgin birth—conception by the Holy Spirit. □ Suffering and death—the facts could be documented. □ Resurrection—eye witnesses saw this. □ Ascension—eye witnesses saw this. □ Second coming—last words of Jesus remembered.

The Apostles Creed was formulated in the second century before the second generation who heard the Apostles' teaching had died off, but its first recorded naming is by Ambrose c.390 A.D.

Jesus Christ

Goal: To examine what you believe about Jesus Christ, the Son of God.

Option 1
RELATIONAL BIBLE STUDY
Who Am I?
In groups of 4, read the Scripture aloud and discuss the questions, one at a time.

> *When Jesus came to the region of Caesarea Philippi, he asked his disciples, "Who do people say the Son of Man is?"*
> *They replied, "Some say John the Baptist; others say Elijah; and still others, Jeremiah or one of the prophets."*
> *"But what about you?" he asked. "Who do you say I am?"*
> *Simon Peter answered, "You are the Christ, the Son of the living God.". . .*
> *From that time on Jesus began to explain to his disciples that he must go to Jerusalem and suffer many things at the hands of the elders, chief priests and teachers of the law, and that he must be killed and on the third day be raised to life.*
> *Peter took him aside and began to rebuke him. "Never, Lord!" he said. "This shall never happen to you!"*
> *Jesus turned and said to Peter, "Out of my sight, Satan! You are a stumbling block to me; you do not have in mind the things of God, but the things of men."*
> *Then Jesus said to his disciples, "If anyone would come after me, he must deny himself and take up his cross and follow me. For whoever wants to save his life will lose it, but whoever loses his life for me will find it."*   Matthew 16:13-16 and 21-25 NIV

Looking into the Story:

1. If Jesus asked you today, *"Who do the crowds say I am?",* **what would you answer:** (tick three)

_____ the greatest man that ever lived
_____ founder of a religion
_____ good box office
_____ spiritual leader—like Gandhi
_____ stained glass window
_____ swear word
_____ Son of God
_____ kill joy
_____ good man
_____ some power from outer space
_____ close friend
_____ nice guy
_____ social revolutionary
_____ saint—someone I cannot be like

2. When Peter said, *"You are the Christ, the Son of the living God,"* **what was he really saying?**

3. Why did Peter rebuke Jesus? (choose all that apply:)
a. in the circumstances it was a normal reaction
b. his thinking was all the wrong way round
c. he didn't understand Jesus' purpose
d. he didn't understand the Old Testament prophecies about the Messiah
e. he wanted a political kingdom
f. he didn't want to deny himself

Option 2
DEEPER BIBLE STUDY
St. Paul on Jesus

In his letter to the young Christians at Colossae (on the northern coast of Greece), St. Paul makes 10 statements about Jesus Christ. Read the passage in the LEFT COLUMN and respond to the statement in the RIGHT COLUMN by circling A if you AGREE, D if you DISAGREE, and ? if not sure..

ABOUT CHRIST	THE DIFFERENCE JESUS MAKES IN MY LIFE
"He [Christ] is the image of the invisible God ..."	A D ? To know Jesus Christ is to know God because Jesus is the exact likeness of God.
"... the firstborn over all creation...."	A D ? To know Jesus is to be personally related to the one who has been in on everything from the beginning.
"For by him [Christ] all things were created; things in heaven and on earth, visible and invisible, whether thrones or powers or rulers or authorities."	A D ? To know Jesus Christ is to know the Architect and Creator of the universe.
"All things were created by him [Christ] and for him [Christ]."	A D ? To know Jesus Christ is to have a purpose in life—under his lordship.
"He [Christ] is before all things, and in him all things hold together.	A D ? To know Jesus Christ is to turn over the supervision of my life to the person who sustains the universe.
"And he [Christ] is the head of the body, the church."	A D ? To know Jesus Christ is to be a part of his family on earth—united and bonded together.
"He [Christ] is the beginning and the firstborn from among the dead, so that in everything he might have the supremacy."	A D ? To know Jesus Christ is to be able to look death in the face and say, "I have no fear of you. You are not the end. As Jesus lives, so shall I."
"For God was pleased to have all the fulness dwell in him [Christ]."	A D ? To know Jesus Christ is to be able to draw on his resources at any time.
"And through him to reconcile to himself all things, whether things on earth or things in heaven."	A D ? To know Jesus Christ is to have my friendship with God restored — just as it was meant to be from the beginning.
"... by making peace through his blood, shed on the cross." *Colossians 1:15-20, NIV*	A D ? To know Jesus Christ is to experience God's peace; to work at peace with God, with others, and with myself.

APPLICATION: Take a look at your own spiritual life lately and check where you are:

1. Honestly, what difference does Jesus Christ make in your everyday life right now?
(put a dot on the line)
NOT A WHOLE LOT _____ **EVERYTHING**

2. The spiritual diet that I have been living on lately has been mainly: (circle two)
   a. baby food
   b. TV dinners
   c. meat and potatoes
   d. dehydrated food
   e. junk food

3. To Jesus' invitation to feast on him, my reply is something like:
   a. I'll be there, but I'm on a diet
   b. I'll be there, but I'll have to leave before the dessert
   c. Can I bring my own sandwich?
   d. I'll be there with bells on

CHECKLIST FOR THE LEADER

BEFORE THE SESSION

☐ Coordinator: Prepare the group leaders for questions about the meaning of the passage in the Relational Bible Study.

☐ Group Leaders: Phone your group. Invite them to bring a new person.

☐ Agenda: Choose between the two optional Bible studies. The Relational Bible Study is easier because of the multiple choice questions.

☐ Research: Be prepared to deal with questions about key names or words in the Bible passages, such as John the Baptist, Elijah, Jeremiah, Christ the Son of the living God. Check a commentary.

☐ Ice Breaker: The first question in the Relational Bible Study is the Ice Breaker.

DURING THE SESSION

☐ Welcome: Welcome newcomers. Explain the covenant on page 58 (Leader's Guide). Share the main points in the Introduction.

☐ Divide: Split into groups of 4—in different rooms if possible.

☐ Optional Bible Studies: Choose one. The Relational Bible Study is read aloud and discussed, question by question. The Deeper Bible Study requires a time of silence before you start the sharing.

☐ Application: Save at least 15 minutes for this.

☐ Prayer: Regather for sharing prayer requests and prayer.

AFTER THE SESSION

☐ Group Leaders: Evaluate the session.

☐ Order: Order more books for newcomers from bookshops or S.U. Distribution: 9-11 Clothier Road, Brislington, Bristol BS4 5RL. Telephone (0272) 71907.

INTRODUCTION

The third statement in the Apostles' Creed concerns the Holy Spirit, the third person in the Trinity.

For hundreds of years, the person and work of the Holy Spirit has been neglected in the teaching of the church. Now, suddenly, there is an abundance of interest in the Holy Spirit. When the history of the second half of the 20th century is written, it will probably be called the age of the Holy Spirit.

I believe ... in the Holy Spirit

The person and work of the Holy Spirit can be described in six ways:

1. Creating: The Holy Spirit is the life-giving agent of the Trinity. He was present, along with the Father and the Son, in the creation of the universe and continues to be present in re-creating the universe.

2. Conceiving: The Holy Spirit was the agent of conception with Mary, the mother of Jesus.

3. Revealing: The Holy Spirit is the agent of the Trinity in revealing divine truth, particularly in the inspiration of Scripture, and the interpretation of Scripture to believers today.

4. Convicting: The Holy Spirit is the agent of the Trinity that is active in bringing truth to bear upon the hearts of men, convicting and convincing people of the truth about Jesus Christ.

5. Guiding: The Holy Spirit is active in guiding believers so that together Christians discern God's will.

6. Giving: The Holy Spirit is active in giving special gifts to members in the "body of Christ" for the sake of the "body of Christ."

It is the Holy Spirit who brings about "fruit" in the life of the Christian. This fruit is the natural result of "abiding" in Christ.

In the Last Supper Discourse, John 14-16, Jesus discusses the Holy Spirit's continuing presence in the world — after the ascension of Christ.

The church was given birth 10 days after the ascension when the Holy Spirit "indwelt" the believers at Pentecost. Peter called upon an Old Testament prophecy to explain what happened.

"In the last days, God says,
I will pour out my Spirit on all people.
Your sons and daughters will prophesy,
your young men will see visions,
your old men will dream dreams....' "

Acts 2:14-17, NIV

Holy Spirit

Goal: To examine what you believe about the person and work of the Holy Spirit.

Option 1
RELATIONAL BIBLE STUDY
Famous Last Words

Before you get into the Bible study, take a moment and rank how you would cope with the following stress situations from 1 to 10 — 1 being NO ANXIETY and 10 being HIGH ANXIETY. This might be called your own stress tolerance. If you have actually experienced any of these situations, try to recall the experience when you mark this area.

____ **DEATH: A close friend suddenly dies**
____ **SECURITY: Someone you need and rely on tells you they're leaving**
____ **ACCOMMODATION: You have no where to live after today**
____ **REPUTATION: You risked everything and the cause you believed in turns sour**
____ **FRIENDS: Old friends move away**
____ **SUICIDE: An acquaintance commits suicide**
____ **BETRAYAL: You feel let down by the one person in the world you trusted**
____ **SHAME: Your judgment is proved wrong and people laugh at you**
____ **HOPE: The dreams you have built for the future are shattered**

Now, read the passage below and discuss the questions under "Looking into the Story."

> *"I will ask the Father, and he will give you another Counselor [Helper], to be with you forever—the Spirit of truth. The world cannot accept him [this Counselor], because it neither sees him nor knows him. But you know him, for he lives with you and will be in you. I will not leave you as orphans.... But the Counselor, the Holy Spirit, whom the Father will send in my name, will teach you all things and will remind you of everything I have said to you. Peace I leave with you; my peace I give you. I do not give to you as the world gives. Do not let your hearts be troubled and do not be afraid."*
>
> *John 14:16-18, 26-27, NIV*

Looking into the Story:

1. How do you think the people in the room at that time felt when they heard the news that Jesus would be leaving them? (Tick two)

☐ all excited
☐ totally depressed
☐ they didn't believe it
☐ terrified/scared to death
☐ relieved
☐ completely mystified
☐ like hiding/crawling into a hole
☐ confused/bewildered
☐ other _____

2. What do you think the disciples needed most in their lives at this moment? (List top 3)

____ **Teacher:** Someone to remind them of God's words/sharpen their understanding
____ **Counselor:** Someone to give direction to their lives
____ **Comforter:** Someone to care for their hurts/pain/desolation
____ **Friend:** Someone who would never leave them
____ **Overcomer:** Someone to give power and strength to their lives
____ **Peace:** Someone to bring deep, abiding peace to their shattered lives

My Own Story:

1. If you were facing the same crisis that the disciples faced, would your faith hold up?
   a. Yes, my faith has been through rougher storms before
   b. No, I don't think my faith right now would hold up
   c. I don't know what I'd do
   d. Ask me tomorrow

2. Of the special ministries of the Holy Spirit that are described in the Scripture passage, which ministry do you especially need for the area above where you indicated your "High Anxiety"?

   □ Teacher   □ Counselor   □ Comforter
   □ Friend   □ Overcomer   □ Peace

3. How active is the Holy Spirit right now in directing your life? (Put a dot on the line to indicate the relationship.)

Inactive _____ Highly active

Option 2
DEEPER BIBLE STUDY
The Fruit of the Spirit (see Galatians 5:22-26)
The Apostle Paul describes a person who is living "in" the Spirit as a person who is "full" of the fruit of the Spirit. How is the fruit of the Spirit ripening in your life?

   In silence, circle a number from 1 to 10 — 1 being very little evidence and 10 being lots of evidence — for each fruit. Then, get together in groups of 4 and share two fruits: (a) the fruit where you ranked yourself closest to 1 and (b) the fruit where you ranked yourself closest to 10.

LOVE: Unconditional acceptance of others, no strings attached, no anticipated "payoff," no attempt to control or manipulate others—especially those you love the most.
1 2 3 4 5 6 7 8 9 10

JOY: Spontaneous, effervescent cheerfulness, flowing from deep spiritual reservoirs—especially in times of stress.
1 2 3 4 5 6 7 8 9 10

PEACE: Inner harmony, soundness, well-being, at-one-ment with God that makes possible a spirit of reconciliation in the midst of conflict, especially in your family.
1 2 3 4 5 6 7 8 9 10

PATIENCE: Strength of will in the midst of trying circumstances and exasperating people—not easily threatened when things don't go your way.
1 2 3 4 5 6 7 8 9 10

KINDNESS: Sensitivity and compassion for those who are hurting, sympathy and empathy for those who are having a bad day—especially those in your own family.
1 2 3 4 5 6 7 8 9 10

GOODNESS: Disposition to do what is right, fair, honorable, and honest; integrity; 14-carat character; champion of truth, justice, and principles—even if you have to stand alone or against your friends.
1 2 3 4 5 6 7 8 9 10

FAITHFULNESS: unwavering, constant, genuine fidelity to what you value, believe and cherish—being true to yourself at the cost of friends, job, and reputation.
1 2 3 4 5 6 7 8 9 10

HUMILITY: Genuine meekness (not weakness), gentleness, tenderness. Healthy self-esteem that does not have to put on airs or try to impress anyone—ANYONE—especially those you are thinking of right now.
1 2 3 4 5 6 7 8 9 10

SELF-CONTROL: Aware of your strengths and weaknesses; in control of your doubts or illusions of grandeur; open to the Spirit but suspicious of your motives; master of your physical/sexual desires.
1 2 3 4 5 6 7 8 9 10

AFFIRMATION: Now, go back over the list above and think of the others in your group. In silence, jot down the names of the others in your group next to the particular "fruit" where you see this person is strongest. For example, you might put Jane's name next to "Faithfulness" because you have observed her constancy and loyalty.

HOW TO SHARE: Ask one person to sit in silence while the others explain where they jotted down this person's name and why. Then, ask the next person to remain silent while you "affirm" this person.

CHECKLIST FOR THE LEADER

BEFORE THE SESSION

□ Coordinator: Go over the teaching on the Holy Spirit in the Introduction with the Group Leaders. Note the context of the Scripture passage—the Last Supper.

□ Group Leaders: Phone your group to see how they are.

□ Lesson plan: Decide which Bible study to use.

□ Deeper Bible Study: The end of the sharing is an "Affirmation" exercise—where one person sits in silence while the others share the "fruit" they have observed. Practise this in your training session.

DURING THE SESSION

□ Welcome: Welcome newcomers. Explain the covenant on page 58 (Leader's Guide).

□ Introduce: Set the stage for the Bible study by explaining the topic — the Holy Spirit — and the background to the Bible passage you have chosen.

□ Divide: Split into groups of 4, preferably in different rooms.

□ Relational Bible Study: It starts off with a Coping Test.

□ Deeper Bible Study: If you have time, reverse the sharing process. Have one person sit in silence while the others "affirm" the Fruit they have observed in this person's life, etc. (see page 51 AFFIRMATION.)

□ Prayer: Regather for prayer, remembering each other's prayer requests.

AFTER THE SESSION

□ Group Leaders: Evaluate the session.

□ Order: Order more books for newcomers from bookshops or S.U. Distribution: 9-11 Clothier Road, Brislington, Bristol BS4 5RL. Telephone (0272) 71907.

INTRODUCTION

The fourth statement in the Apostles Creed concerns the church.

"I believe . . . in the holy catholic church, the communion of the saints."

The word *church* means "to call out." It can refer to any assembly of people; but the two words "holy" and "catholic" help to clarify the meaning.

The word *holy* comes from the Hebrew word "to be separate". It usually is associated with God. When it is associated with people, it refers to a people that God set apart for a special relationship with Himself. In the New Testament, the believers are called a "holy temple"—set apart for a special function.

The word *catholic* means "universal". It refers to the "oneness" that all believers have "in Christ". The Apostle Paul calls the believers the "body of Christ"—brought together by a common "baptism" through the Holy Spirit.

I believe in the communion of the saints

The Apostles' Creed further defines the church as a "communion of saints". The word *saint* means one who has been "set apart"; and the word *"communion"* means fellowship. Thus, the church is further described as a fellowship between those who have been set apart by the call of God for a new "family"—the family of God.

The church had its beginning with Pentecost when the Holy Spirit entered into the followers of Jesus as he had promised before his ascension, making the followers of Christ into a family—a very special family that Paul called "the body of Christ."

The New Testament describes the church as: □ the bride of Christ, □ a holy temple, □a royal priesthood, □ a holy nation, □ the body of Christ.

The Parable of the Frog

Once upon a time there was a frog. . . .
But he wasn't really a frog.
He was a prince who looked and felt like a frog.
A wicked witch had cast a spell on him and only
    the kiss of a beautiful maiden could save him.
But no one wanted to kiss this frog!
So there he sat—an unkissed prince in frog form.
But . . . one day along came a beautiful maiden
    who gave this frog a great big smack.
    Crash—Boom—Zap!
There he was—a handsome, dashing prince.
(And you know the rest—they lived happily ever
    after).
So what is the task of the church?
To kiss frogs, of course!!
                    —Wes Seeliger

Session 4

The Church Universal

Goal: To examine what you believe about the church.

Option 1
RELATIONAL BIBLE STUDY
Life Together

Read over the description of the early church in Acts 2:42-47 and measure your own church (and more particularly, your present Bible study group) against these six characteristics. Circle a number from 1 to 10—1 being very weak and 10 being very strong—under each category. Then, get together in groups of 4 and share your results.

> *They devoted themselves to the apostles' teaching and to the fellowship, to the breaking of bread and to prayer. Everyone was filled with awe, and many wonders and miraculous signs were done by the apostles. All the believers were together and had everything in common. Selling their possessions and goods, they gave to anyone as he had need. Every day they continued to meet together in the temple courts. They broke bread in their homes and ate together with glad and sincere hearts, praising God and enjoying the favor of all the people. And the Lord added to their number daily those who were being saved.*
> Acts 2:42-47, NIV

1. SPIRITUAL NURTURE/GROWTH: *"They devoted themselves to the apostles' teaching and to the fellowship, to the breaking of bread and to prayer."*

We give PRIORITY to studying the Scripture, to meeting with other believers for the purpose of learning more about our faith and to pray for one another.

1 2 3 4 5 6 7 8 9 10

2. SPIRITUAL HEALING: *"Everyone was filled with awe, and many wonders and miraculous signs were done by the apostles."*

We expect and anticipate the healing ministry of the Holy Spirit in our midst, and we see God's healing power in people and relationships all the time.

1 2 3 4 5 6 7 8 9 10

3. SPIRITUAL CARING: *"All the believers were together and had everything in common. Selling their possessions and goods, they gave to anyone as he had need."*

There are no needs in our fellowship because we look after one another. If someone is out of food, out of work, or in need in other ways, we do what we can to support each other.

1 2 3 4 5 6 7 8 9 10

4. CORPORATE WORSHIP: *"Every day they continued to meet together in the temple courts."*

We meet regularly for worship with the larger body of believers—to celebrate Christ's resurrection and His triumph over sin.

1 2 3 4 5 6 7 8 9 10

5. SMALL SHARING GROUPS: *"They broke bread in their homes and ate together with glad and sincere hearts, praising God and enjoying the favor of all the people."*

We also meet regularly in small Bible study and support groups to praise God, study the Bible, share our needs, and support one another.

1 2 3 4 5 6 7 8 9 10

6. NUMERICAL GROWTH: *"And the Lord added to their number daily those who were being saved."*

We keep our groups open to new people that have become believers and need a Bible study and support group . . . and the Lord continues to add to our number each week.

1 2 3 4 5 6 7 8 9 10

Option 2
DEEPER BIBLE STUDY
Body Building

Right after the instruction from the Apostle Paul to the young Christians in Rome to "find the will of God" for their lives (Romans 12:2), he proceeds to give a list of seven "spiritual gifts" that are distributed to the church—the body of Christ.

One of the best ways for "finding the will of God" for your life is to study the 7 spiritual gifts — to share with others and see where you best exercise your ministry within the body of Christ.

Seven Gifts

Read over the entire passage for the context. Then, study the 7 gifts—described in terms of people. Which personality comes closest to your personality?

When you have finished, get together in groups of 8 and share what you have come up with: (a) how you see your own "gift" and (b) how you see the others in your community.

> *"Do not conform any longer to the pattern of this world, but be transformed by the renewing of your mind. Then you will be able to test and approve what God's will is— his good, pleasing and perfect will. . . . .Just as each of us has one body with many members, and these members do not all have the same function, so in Christ we who are many form one body, and each member belongs to all the others. We have different gifts, according to the grace given us. If a man's gift is PROPHESYING, let him use it in proportion to his faith. If it is SERVING, let him serve; if it is TEACHING, let him teach; if it is ENCOURAGING, let him encourage; if it is CONTRIBUTING (GIVING) to the needs of others, let him give generously; if it is LEADERSHIP (ADMINISTERING), let him govern diligently; if it is showing MERCY (sympathy), let him do it cheerfully."*
> Romans 12:2, 4-8 NIV (CAPS ADDED)

SPIRITUAL GIFTS (tick the one closest to your basic personality).

☐ **THE PROPHET: Talk-oriented.** Forthright, outspoken, and strongwilled. A natural-born leader. Good talker/poor listener. Dogmatic, strong convictions, uncompromising. Sometimes hard to live with; insensitive to other's feelings, hardnosed, and a little overpowering.

☐ **THE SERVANT: Practical-needs-oriented.** Hardworking, conscientious, and faithful. Natural-born helper—behind the scenes. Gets satisfaction out of seeing things done, regardless of who gets the credit. Often gets overextended and overworked to the neglect of his or her own spiritual life. Can be "self pitying" and "bitchy."

☐ **THE TEACHER: Concept-oriented.** Systematic, logical, and theoretical. A natural-born word processor. Good at careful, painstaking research, organizing data, and writing books and sermons— sometimes interesting. Can get a little "stuffy," cloistered, unrelated to people and even a little "proud" of accomplishments.

☐ **THE ENCOURAGER: Success-oriented.** Self-disciplined, single-minded, completely dedicated. Good at setting goals and helping others achieve their goals. Can be a little demanding, hard on self . . . and hard on others, particularly when results aren't readily seen. Easily discouraged when his or her expectations are not fulfilled.

☐ **THE GIVER (PHILANTHROPIST): Cause-oriented.** Analyst, strategist, natural-born investment broker. Able to see the "big picture," assess resources, accumulate wealth and use it wisely. Easily upset by the misuse of time, talent, and resources in the church. Desperately needed, but seldom appreciated.

☐ **THE ADMINISTRATOR: Task-oriented.** Organized, authoritative, decisive, and thrives under pressure. Good at delegating responsibility and getting things done through others. Can be a little insensitive, manipulative, and "pushy" when the task demands it.

☐ **THE SYMPATHIZER: Feeling-oriented.** Highly sensitive to others in need, compassionate and affirming. Good at listening, caring, and "being present" when someone is hurting. This kind of person can be easily "hurt," emotionally drained, and/or make people "dependent" on them.

CHECKLIST FOR THE LEADER

BEFORE THE SESSION

☐ Coordinator: Prepare the group leaders for the topic "Church Universal," and the meaning of "spiritual gifts" in Romans 12 (Deeper Bible Study).

☐ Group Leaders: Decide which Bible study to use. If you go with the Deeper Bible study, do some research on the Romans 12 passage about "spiritual gifts."

☐ Parable of Frog: Discuss what you can learn from the poem about the frog.

☐ Plan Ahead: What are you going to suggest to the Bible study group after this unit?

DURING THE SESSION

☐ Welcome: Welcome newcomers. Explain the covenant on page 58 (Leader's Guide).

☐ Introduction: Read the parable of the frog in the Introduction.

☐ Divide: Split into groups of 4, in different rooms.

☐ Relational Bible Study: You can look at the evaluation test from two perspectives: (a) your entire church or (b) your small Bible study group.

☐ Deeper Bible Study: Explain the background for the Romans passage and allow everyone to complete the exercise in silence before starting to share.

☐ Prayer: Regather for sharing prayer requests and prayer at the close.

AFTER THE SESSION

☐ Group Leaders: Evaluate the session.

☐ Think Ahead: Discuss studying the Advanced courses.

☐ New Groups: Start some new groups or split your groups to allow for multiplication when you move into the Advanced Units.

INTRODUCTION

The fifth statement in the Apostles Creed deals with the problem of sin.

"I believe . . . in the forgiveness of sin."

In the English language, we have only one word for sin. In the original Biblical languages, however, there were many words. If we could understand the Biblical words for sin, we could clear up a lot of the misunderstandings that divide Christians today.

Teachers of doctrine usually stress the words that emphasize the sinful NATURE OF MAN — dwelling on the Hebrew words AWA (bent, twisted, wrung out of shape) and AWAL (iniquity, lacking in integrity).

The more experience-centered teachers usually emphasize the sinful ACTS OF SIN that result from the sinful nature — dwelling on the Hebrew words AVAR (transgression, crossing over the boundary) and PASHA (wilful disobedience, rebellion).

The more evangelistic preachers usually go heavy on the CONSEQUENCES OF SIN — dwelling on the Hebrew words AMAL (travail, pain, suffering); RA (alienation, disruption, ruin) and RASHA (tossing, agitation, restlessness).

The point is—ALL THREE SCHOOLS OF THOUGHT ARE RIGHT. Sin refers to a NATURE that is bent, twisted, and slightly off course that is inherited from the "fall" of mankind; the nature results in ACTS of sin that fall short of the mark and deliberate disobedience; and the acts of sin bring about CONSEQUENCES that include alienation from God, restlessness, and finally destruction and death.

I believe . . . in the forgiveness of sin

The good news of the gospel is that God has made an "atonement" for sin. In the Old Testament, atonement meant "to cover" with the sacrifice of an innocent animal. In the New Testament, "atonement" took on a new meaning in the person and work of Jesus Christ. "Behold the Lamb of God who TAKES AWAY the sin of the world."

The good news is that Jesus Christ has made a complete payment for the sin and I do not have to pay for my own sin any more.

"If we confess our sins, he is faithful and just and will forgive us our sins and purify us from all unrighteousness." 1 John 1:9, NIV

Session 5

The Forgiveness of Sins

Goal: To examine what you believe about the meaning of sin and the basis on which God forgives sin.

Option 1
RELATIONAL BIBLE STUDY
Pharisee or Tax Collector
Divide into groups of 4. Then, read the passage together and discuss the questions, one at a time.

> To some who were confident of their own righteousness and looked down on everybody else, Jesus told this parable: "Two men went up to the temple to pray, one a Pharisee and the other a tax collector. The Pharisee stood up and prayed about himself: 'God, I thank you that I am not like all other men—robbers, evildoers, adulterers—or even like this tax collector. I fast twice a week and give a tenth of all I get.'
>
> "But the tax collector stood at a distance. He would not even look up to heaven, but beat his breast and said, 'God, have mercy on me, a sinner.'
>
> "I tell you that this man, rather than the other, went home justified before God. For everyone who exalts himself will be humbled, and he who humbles himself will be exalted."
>
> Luke 18:9-14, NIV

Looking into the Story:

1. Why did Jesus tell this parable?
   a. to make Pharisees look bad
   b. to give tax collectors a pat on the back
   c. to show what righteousness was not
   d. to show what it takes to get right with God
   e. to show how Pharisees had turned people off

2. Why do you think the Pharisee acted the way he did?
   a. he was over scrupulous
   b. peer pressure from his religious friends
   c. sincere effort to please God
   d. attempt to cover up what he knew he was really like
   e. a wrong view of what really pleases God

3. Why do you think the tax collector acted the way he did?
   a. he didn't know any better
   b. he had nothing to boast about
   c. he knew he had done wrong
   d. he wanted sympathy
   e. his past had caught up with him

4. Why did Jesus say that the tax collector went home justified (forgiven)?
   a. he gave back all the money he had taken from the people
   b. he left his job
   c. he started going to church every day
   d. he felt sincerely sorry for his wrongdoing
   e. he asked God for mercy and God forgave him

My Own Story

1. If this incident really happened on the steps of your church, who would you feel closest to?   ☐ Pharisee   ☐ Tax collector

2. How much of your own problems could you share with these two people? Put a dot on the lines below somewhere in between NOTHING and ANYTHING.

With the Pharisee, I could share . . .
NOTHING _____ ANYTHING

With the tax collector, I could share . . .
NOTHING _____ ANYTHING

3. How much of the Pharisee and tax collector do you see in your own life at two different periods: (a) Five years ago and (b) right now. Put a percentage (%) for each part of you. (The two percentages must add up to 100 percent.)

FIVE YEARS AGO, I WAS _____% PHARISEE AND _____% TAX COLLECTOR.

RIGHT NOW, I AM PROBABLY _____% PHARISEE AND _____% TAX COLLECTOR.

Option 2
DEEPER BIBLE STUDY
All This and Heaven Too

What are the results of God's forgiveness? Here are a few things that are true of all Christians. Read over the statement and the passage that explains it . . . and then put an "x" on the line below the passage to indicate your own response — somewhere between NO and YES.

I AM MADE A NEW PERSON—A NEW CREATION

"Therefore, if anyone is in Christ, he is a new creation; the old has gone, the new has come!" 2 Corinthians 5:17 NIV
NO _____ YES

I AM RECONCILED: That is, my broken relationship with God has been healed. My friendship with God is restored; I am to help others to be reconciled.

"All this is from God, who reconciled us to himself through Christ and gave us the ministry of reconciliation: that God was reconciling the world to himself in Christ, not counting men's sins against them." 2 Corinthians 5:18-19
NO _____ YES

I AM JUSTIFIED: That is, the sentence of death that was hanging over my head has been taken away because Christ took my place . . . and I have been given a pardon.

"Therefore, since we have been justified through faith [in Christ], we have peace with God through our Lord Jesus Christ, through whom we have gained access by faith into this grace in which we now stand." Romans 5:1-2 NIV
NO _____ YES

I AM CHOSEN: That is, I have been selected to have a share in God's blessings.

"Praise be to the God and Father of our Lord Jesus Christ, who has blessed us in the heavenly realms with every spiritual blessing in Christ. For he chose us in him [Christ] before the creation of the world to be holy and blameless in his sight." Ephesians 1:3-4 NIV
NO _____ YES

I AM ADOPTED: That is, I have been brought into his family with all of the rights and privileges of a son.
"In love he [God] predestined us to be adopted as his sons through Jesus Christ, in accordance with his pleasure and will— to the praise of his glorious grace . . . ." Ephesians 1:5-6 NIV
NO _____ YES

I AM REDEEMED: That is, the payment for my sin has been paid (by Christ) and I am free to serve my new master—Jesus Christ.

"In him [Christ] we have redemption through his [Christ's] blood . . . " Ephesians 1:7
"Jesus Christ, who gave himself for us to redeem us from all wickedness and to purify for himself a people that are his very own, eager to do what is good." Titus 2:14
NO _____ YES

I AM A CITIZEN OF HEAVEN: That is, I have been given a new allegiance.

"Consequently, you are no longer foreigners and aliens, but fellow citizens with God's people and members of God's household, built on the foundation of the apostles and prophets, with Christ Jesus himself as the chief cornerstone." Ephesians 2:19-20 NIV
NO _____ YES

I AM A VERY SPECIAL PERSON: That is, I have been given a new calling as part of the purpose and plan of God.

"But you are a chosen people, a royal priesthood, a holy nation, a people belonging to God, that you may declare the praises of him who called you out of darkness into his wonderful light." 1 Peter 2:9 NIV
NO _____ YES

CHECKLIST FOR THE LEADER

BEFORE THE SESSION

☐ Coordinator: In your training session with Group Leaders, go over the teaching on Sin and the basis for Forgiveness. Also, discuss the future plans for groups.

☐ Group Leaders: Be prepared to deal with deep questions about the meaning of sin, guilt, and forgiveness. Emphasise God's grace and forgiveness.

☐ Optional Bible Studies: Choose which study to use.

☐ Closing Party: Plan something to celebrate the completion of the "Trial" period of the Bible study group. Invite spouses, friends, and kids and use one of the Socials on pages 73-95.

DURING THE SESSION

☐ Welcome: Welcome newcomers. Explain the covenant on page 58 (Leader's Guide).

☐ Introduction: Explain the topic and the three aspects of "sin" in the special box.

☐ Divide: Split into groups of 4, preferably in separate rooms.

☐ Relational Bible Study: Simply read the Bible passage and start on the questions.

☐ Deeper Bible Study: Complete the exercise in silence before starting on the sharing.

☐ Prayer: Regather for prayer at the close.

AFTER THE SESSION

☐ Group Leaders: Evaluate the session.

☐ Social: Plan a social (See pages 73-95).

☐ Next Steps: Decide if you want to continue with the Advanced course.

INTRODUCTION

The last two statements in the Apostles' Creed deal with the resurrection of Jesus Christ and our own hope of life everlasting.

"I believe . . . in the resurrection of the body and life everlasting."

The bodily resurrection of Jesus Christ from the dead has historically been the cornerstone of the Christian faith. The early Christians were transformed from a defeated, despairing, hopeless band of followers of a guru that claimed to be the Messiah into a bold, fearless, band of "witnesses" to the physical resurrection of their leader from the dead.

The religious establishment tried to threaten these followers with persecution. The Roman authorities actually carried out repeated attempts to annihilate the Christians in the first three centuries. But all their efforts only succeeded in fanning the flame in the spread of Christianity.

Doubting Thomas

The first doubter of the resurrection was one of the twelve disciples, whom Jesus scolded for his statement: "Unless I see the nail marks in his hands and put my finger where the nails were, and put my hand into his side, I will not believe." John 20:25 NIV

Through the centuries, sceptics have arisen who have questioned the "bodily" resurrection. Some have taught that Jesus never really died— that he was revived when they put him in the tomb. Others have taught that the soul of Jesus came back to life, but not the body.

Against these false teachings, the Apostle Paul reasserted the bodily resurrection of Jesus Christ as the proof that believers will also conquer death:

"Now, brothers, I want to remind you of the gospel I preached to you, which you received and on which you have taken your stand. By this gospel you are saved, if you hold firmly to the word I preached to you. Otherwise, you have believed in vain.

"For what I received I passed on to you as of first importance: that Christ died for our sins according to the Scriptures, that he was buried, that he was raised on the third day according to the Scriptures, and that he appeared to Peter, and then to the Twelve. After that, he appeared to more than five hundred of the brothers at the same time, most of whom are still living, though some have fallen asleep. Then he appeared to James, then to all the apostles, and last of all he appeared to me also, as to one abnormally born." 1 Corinthians 15:1-8, NIV

Resurrection and Life Everlasting

Goal: To examine what you believe on the bodily resurrection of Jesus Christ and life everlasting.

Option 1
RELATIONAL BIBLE STUDY
Doubting Thomas

Divide into groups of 4. Read the passage together and discuss the questions, one at a time.

> *Now Thomas (called Didymus), one of the Twelve, was not with the disciples when Jesus came. When the other disciples told him that they had seen the Lord, he declared, "Unless I see the nail marks in his hands and put my finger where the nails were, and put my hand into his side, I will not believe it."*
>
> *A week later his disciples were in the house again, and Thomas was with them. Though the doors were locked, Jesus came and stood among them and said, "Peace be with you!" Then he said to Thomas, "Put your finger here; see my hands. Reach out your hand and put it into my side. Stop doubting and believe."*
>
> *Thomas said to him, "My Lord and my God!"*
>
> *Then Jesus told him, "Because you have seen me, you have believed; blessed are those who have not seen and yet have believed."*
>   *John 20:24-29, NIV*

Looking into the Story

1. If I had been one of the disciples of Jesus right after his death, I probably would have been:
   a. hiding, too
   b. completely disillusioned
   c. terrified
   d. brokenhearted
   e. sceptical about everything
   f. other _____

2. When Thomas said, *"Unless I see the nail marks in his hands and put my finger where the nails were, and put my hand into his side, I will not believe it,"* he was really saying:
   a. "Prove it"
   b. "Show me"
   c. "You're crazy"
   d. "I want to believe, but . . ."
   e. "Don't break my heart any more . . ."
   f. " _____ "

3. Jesus dealt with Thomas' question by:
   a. gently rebuking him
   b. making him look faithless
   c. giving him the evidence he asked for
   d. excluding him from the group
   e. other _____

4. When Thomas discovered that Jesus was really alive, he was:
   a. ashamed
   b. convinced
   c. a little sheepish
   d. ecstatic/overjoyed
   e. other _____

My Own Story

1. In my own quest for religious certainty, I am the kind who relies on:
   a. simple faith
   b. logic
   c. Bible
   d. historical evidence
   e. scientific verification
   f. my minister/priest
   g. what feels right

2. The thing that helps me to believe in the resurrection is:
   a. the fact that the Bible says so
   b. the evidence of daily miracles
   c. the faith of my parents
   d. the historical endurance of the church
   e. experiencing his presence in this support group and other places
   f. my own life change

Option 2
DEEPER BIBLE STUDY
Pick a Promise to Grow On

Look down the road a few years and pick a promise from the collection below for the next step in your journey.

Then, evaluate your experience during this course and share in groups of 4 where you have grown.

Finally, get everyone together and celebrate your experience.

THE PROMISES OF GOD

☐ *... I am sure that God, who began this good work in you, will carry it on until it is finished on the Day of Christ Jesus.*
Philippians 1:6, GNB

☐ *Call to me, and I will answer you; I will tell you wonderful and marvelous things that you know nothing about.*
Jeremiah 33:3, GNB

☐ *Do not cling to events of the past or dwell on what happened long ago. Watch for the new thing I am going to do. It is happening already—you can see it now! I will make a road through the wilderness and give you streams of water there.*
Isaiah 43:18-19, GNB

☐ *And God is able to give you more than you need, so that you will always have all you need for yourselves and more than enough for every good cause.*
2 Corinthians 9:8, GNB

☐ *I have the strength to face all conditions by the power that Christ gives me.*
Philippians 4:13, GNB

☐ *When anyone is joined to Christ, he is a new being; the old is gone, the new has come.*
2 Corinthians 5:17, GNB

☐ *We know that in all things God works for good with those who love him, those whom he has called according to his purpose.*
Romans 8:28, GNB

☐ *Those who trust in the Lord for help will find their strength renewed. They will rise on wings like eagles; they will run and not get weary; they will walk and not grow weak.*
Isaiah 40:31, GNB

☐ *Ask, and you will receive; seek, and you will find; knock, and the door will be opened to you. For everyone who asks will receive, and anyone who seeks will find, and the door will be opened to him who knocks.*
Matthew 7:7, GNB

☐ *Every test that you have experienced is the kind that normally comes to people. But God keeps his promise, and he will not allow you to be tested beyond your power to remain firm; at the time you are put to the test, he will give you the strength to endure it, and so provide you with a way out.*
1 Corinthians 10:13, GNB

☐ *Listen! I stand at the door and knock; if anyone hears my voice and opens the door, I will come into his house and eat with him, and he will eat with me.*
Revelation 3:20, GNB

☐ *Who ... can separate us from the love of Christ? Can trouble do it, or hardship or persecution or hunger or poverty or danger or death?... No, in all these things we have complete victory through him who loved us! For I am certain that nothing can separate us from his love: neither death nor life, neither angels nor other heavenly rulers or powers, neither the present nor the future, neither the world above nor the world below—there is nothing in all creation that will ever be able to separate us from the love of God which is ours through Christ Jesus our Lord.*
Romans 8:35-38, GNB

☐ *I will always guide you and satisfy you with good things. I will keep you strong and well. You will be like a garden that has plenty of water, like a spring of water that never goes dry.*
Isaiah 58:11, GNB

CHECKLIST FOR THE LEADER

BEFORE THE SESSION

☐ Coordinator: With your Group Leaders, decide on the next phase of the Bible study groups. Either integrate new people into existing groups as they move to the Advanced level ... or start new groups for newcomers at the Beginner level.

☐ Group Leaders: Plan some time for summing up at the close of the session—for everyone to share where they have grown.

☐ Party: Plan something special to celebrate the time together. (See the party options on pages 73-95, especially the "Going Away Party" on page 94).

DURING THE SESSION

☐ Welcome: Welcome newcomers. Explain the covenant on page 58 (Leader's Guide).

☐ Introduce: The final statement in the Apostles Creed.

☐ Divide: Split into groups of 4, preferably in different rooms.

☐ Relational Bible Study: Explain that the Bible passage comes after the death and resurrection of Christ.

☐ Deeper Bible Study: The exercise is designed especially for evaluation.

☐ Prayer: Regather all of the groups for a time of celebration, evaluation, and praise.

AFTER THE SESSION

☐ Group leaders: Evaluate the session and the whole unit. How has your group developed? Decide what course to study for the future.

I believe in GOD, the Father Almighty, Creator of heaven and earth:
I believe in JESUS CHRIST his only Son our Lord. He was conceived by the power of the Holy Spirit and born of the Virgin Mary.
He suffered under Pontius Pilate, was crucified, died and was buried.
He descended to the dead. On the third day he rose again. He ascended into heaven, and is seated at the right hand of the Father. He will come again to judge the living and the dead.
I believe in the HOLY SPIRIT: the holy catholic CHURCH, the communion of saints, the FORGIVENESS OF SINS, the RESURRECTION of the body, and the LIFE EVERLASTING.

Amen. *Apostles Creed*

Families

8 MONTHLY GET TOGETHER PROGRAMMES FOR YOUR EXTENDED FAMILY

FAMILIES

Kids' (of all ages) Party

(Anyone under 95 gets in free)

THEME: Games we used to play

DRESS: Casual

SETTING: Indoors / church hall

FOOD: Each family brings a main course and a sweet to be shared

PURPOSE: Get to know each other's spouses and kids

PROGRAMME: Choose one or two games in each category. Tension Breakers for whole group. Team Relays to combine two families OR to divide up families. The BIG Game played with same teams.

EQUIPMENT:

☐ Stick-on name tags / felt pens

☐ Photocopy Bingo card / pencil for everyone

☐ Game on next page for each team, plus a dice or spinner

☐ Special equipment for games you choose

Jokes

While everyone is eating, see if someone can guess the answers to these jokes. (Answers on the next page.)

1. What do you have when you cross a chicken and a clock?
2. What did the first ghost say to the second ghost?
3. If a rooster lays an egg on the peak of a roof, which way will the egg roll?
4. What happens when you tickle a mule?
5. Did you hear the one about the farmer?
6. Why did the elephant leave the zoo?
7. What do you call a dog with no legs?
8. Where does steel wool come from?
9. Who's bigger, Mrs. Bigger or her baby?
10. What's yellow and highly dangerous?

Tension Breakers (Whole group)

To break the ice and get everyone (especially the kids and spouses) acquainted, here are three tension breakers. Choose one or two and collect the necessary equipment.

BINGO

Equipment: Bingo card below and pencil for everyone.

Give Bingo card and pencil to everyone. At the word GO, everyone mills around, asking one person at a time ONE question on card. If this person answers "Yes," write their first name in box. This person, in turn, gets to ask you ONE question. If you answer "yes," this person puts your first name in that box.

After one question each, you *must* move on to another person. Ask a question and if their answer is "yes," write their first name in the box.

uses Crest toothpaste	talk to myself in public	reads "Peanuts"	saves stamps	loves peanut butter	shave my legs
plays chess regularly	can whistle "Danny Boy"	loves Bach	has scar 3 inches long	drove a motorcycle	been camping
ate snails once	picks nose in public	lies about age	has hole in sock now	can touch tongue to nose	can recite books of Bible
listens to "The Archers"	never ridden a horse	can do the Twist	superstitious about ladders	bank account overdrawn now	sings in shower
likes caviar	still have tonsils	broke my leg	detective story fan	watches "Blue Peter"	did not make bed today
can touch their toes	writes poetry	have dyed hair	uses Hai Karate	squeezes toothpaste in middle	eats yoghurt

The first person to fill every box on the card WINS . . . but you cannot have the same name more than _____ (twice or three times, depending on the total number of people at the party).

The first person to fill their Bingo Card should scream BINGO. Then, the leader will stop the game and call off the people named on that card to see if every box is correct. Have fun.

BIRTH DATE TURNOVER
Equipment: None.

This game is similar to the old game "Stations." Have everyone sit in a circle with the same number of chairs as there are people. "It" stands in the centre. This person calls out any number of months of the year. After the last month is called, everyone who has a birthday during one of those months gets up and tries to take another seat. "It" also tries to find a vacant seat. Whoever is left without a seat becomes "it."

HOT POTATO
Equipment: A balloon, bean bag or volleyball.

The players sit in a circle. Someone is selected to be "it" and assumes a position in the centre. "It" is given the "hot potato" which he/she throws at any player in the circle. This person, in turn, throws the "hot potato" to someone else. The object is for the person who is "it" to retrieve the "hot potato." When he/she does, the player responsible must go to the centre and become "it."

Team Relays

Make equal teams by putting two families together or reassigning everyone. Teams should number from 6 to 8 people each, including children.

CHINESE BALLOON CARRY RELAY
Equipment: A large round balloon for each team.

Line up teams behind starting line. Give the first person on each team a large inflated balloon. This person must walk with the balloon between his/her legs to the other end of the room and back again. If

---

Answers to Jokes
1. An alarm cluck.
2. "Do you believe in people?"
3. Roosters don't lay eggs.
4. You get a kick out of it.
5. It's corny.
6. It was tired of working for peanuts.
7. You can call it anything you want but it still won't come to you.
8. Steel sheep.
9. The baby's a little Bigger.
10. Shark-infested custard.

---

the balloon slips out from between their legs, stop and put the balloon back before proceeding. When the first person returns with the balloon, the next person starts, etc. The first team to complete the relay wins.

To add to the fun, also put a book or a paper cup (full of water) on a person's head as he/she walks.

MAGAZINE SCAVENGER HUNT
Equipment: For each team, a complete magazine. Each one should be identical.

Before the game, leaf through the magazine and pick out specific advertisements, photographs, names of famous people, etc. Give this long list to each team leader. On the word GO, the team must find everything on this list . . . and tear it out. Time limit: 5 minutes . . . or the first team to find everything.

Another way to play this game is to call out a word or picture and the first team to bring this item to the centre is the winner.

THREAD THE NEEDLE
Equipment: For each team, a large tablespoon with a 30 foot long string tied around the neck of the spoon.

On the word GO, the first person on each team passes the spoon (with the string tied to it) inside their shirt (or blouse) and one trouser leg . . . and on to the next member of the team. This person, in turn, "threads" the spoon inside his/her clothes . . . and on to the next person, etc., until the spoon has been "threaded" through the whole team.

When the last person has been "threaded," this person begins the process of "unthreading the needle!" This is done by pulling up on the string and getting the "needle" up, through, and out of the slacks and shirt (or whatever). This takes constant teamwork to keep the slack wound up in a neat ball.

The first team to complete the process and wind up the string into a neat ball wins.

The BIG Game *(Next Page)*

Equipment: For *each* team, one game board on the next page and one dice or spinner .
1. Stay with the same teams from the previous games.
2. Give each team a game board (or book) and one dice or spinner.
3. Ask each player to find a "mover," such as a coin, a key, or a lipstick container. Place the "movers" on START.
4. Roll the dice or spinner and advance your mover. If the space requires a demonstration and you can accomplish it, you can move forward again. If the space asks a question, you get to move forward or backward depending on your answer.
5. To finish, you must roll the exact number. The first team to have ALL members of their team to finish WINS.

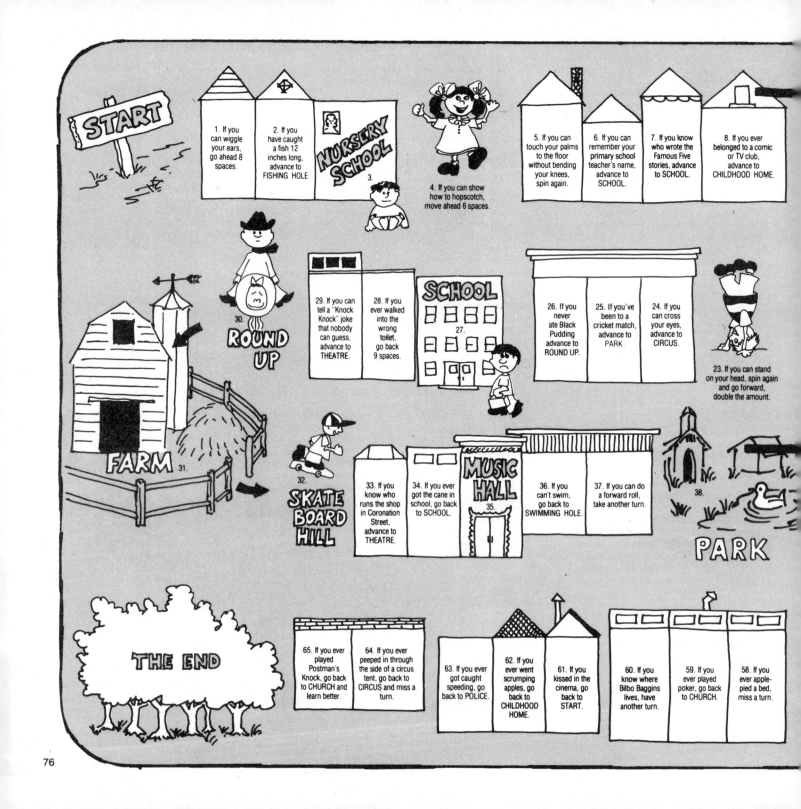

START

1. If you can wiggle your ears, go ahead 8 spaces.

2. If you have caught a fish 12 inches long, advance to FISHING HOLE

NURSERY SCHOOL 3.

4. If you can show how to hopscotch, move ahead 6 spaces.

5. If you can touch your palms to the floor without bending your knees, spin again.

6. If you can remember your primary school teacher's name, advance to SCHOOL.

7. If you know who wrote the Famous Five stories, advance to SCHOOL.

8. If you ever belonged to a comic or TV club, advance to CHILDHOOD HOME.

29. If you can tell a "Knock Knock" joke that nobody can guess, advance to THEATRE.

28. If you ever walked into the wrong toilet, go back 9 spaces.

SCHOOL 27.

26. If you never ate Black Pudding advance to ROUND UP.

25. If you've been to a cricket match, advance to PARK.

24. If you can cross your eyes, advance to CIRCUS.

23. If you can stand on your head, spin again and go forward, double the amount.

ROUND UP 30.

FARM 31.

32.

SKATE BOARD HILL

33. If you know who runs the shop in Coronation Street, advance to THEATRE.

34. If you ever got the cane in school, go back to SCHOOL.

MUSIC HALL 35.

36. If you can't swim, go back to SWIMMING HOLE.

37. If you can do a forward roll, take another turn.

38.

PARK

THE END

65. If you ever played Postman's Knock, go back to CHURCH and learn better.

64. If you ever peeped in through the side of a circus tent, go back to CIRCUS and miss a turn.

63. If you ever got caught speeding, go back to POLICE.

62. If you ever went scrumping apples, go back to CHILDHOOD HOME.

61. If you kissed in the cinema, go back to START.

60. If you know where Bilbo Baggins lives, have another turn.

59. If you ever played poker, go back to CHURCH.

58. If you ever apple-pied a bed, miss a turn.

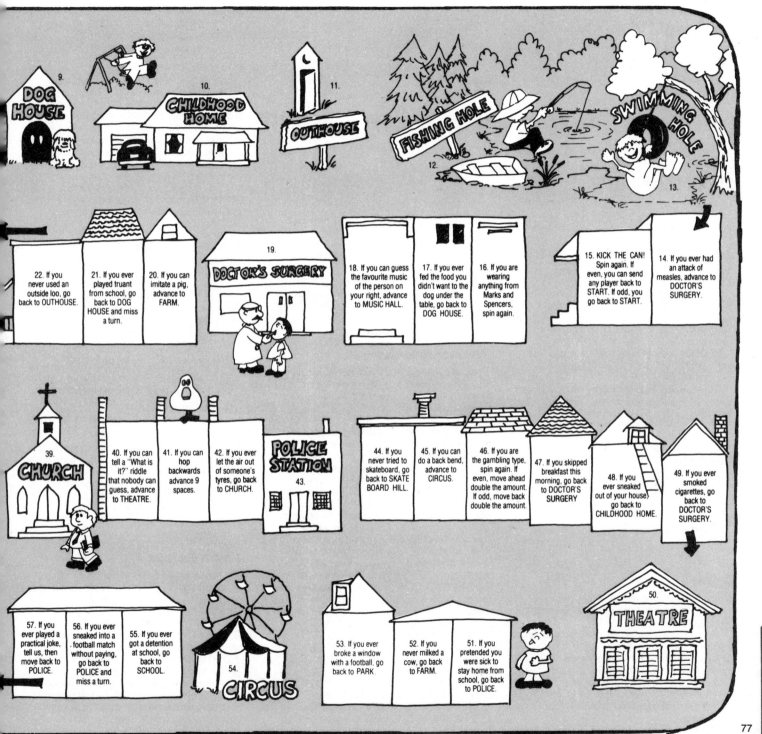

9. DOG HOUSE

10. CHILDHOOD HOME

11. OUTHOUSE

12. FISHING HOLE

13. SWIMMING HOLE

22. If you never used an outside loo, go back to OUTHOUSE.

21. If you ever played truant from school, go back to DOG HOUSE and miss a turn.

20. If you can imitate a pig, advance to FARM.

19. DOCTOR'S SURGERY

18. If you can guess the favourite music of the person on your right, advance to MUSIC HALL.

17. If you ever fed the food you didn't want to the dog under the table, go back to DOG HOUSE.

16. If you are wearing anything from Marks and Spencers, spin again.

15. KICK THE CAN! Spin again. If even, you can send any player back to START. If odd, you go back to START.

14. If you ever had an attack of measles, advance to DOCTOR'S SURGERY.

39. CHURCH

40. If you can tell a "What is it?" riddle that nobody can guess, advance to THEATRE.

41. If you can hop backwards advance 9 spaces.

42. If you ever let the air out of someone's tyres, go back to CHURCH.

43. POLICE STATION

44. If you never tried to skateboard, go back to SKATE BOARD HILL.

45. If you can do a back bend, advance to CIRCUS.

46. If you are the gambling type, spin again. If even, move ahead double the amount. If odd, move back double the amount.

47. If you skipped breakfast this morning, go back to DOCTOR'S SURGERY.

48. If you ever sneaked out of your house, go back to CHILDHOOD HOME.

49. If you ever smoked cigarettes, go back to DOCTOR'S SURGERY.

57. If you ever played a practical joke, tell us, then move back to POLICE.

56. If you ever sneaked into a football match without paying, go back to POLICE and miss a turn.

55. If you ever got a detention at school, go back to SCHOOL.

54. CIRCUS

53. If you ever broke a window with a football, go back to PARK.

52. If you never milked a cow, go back to FARM.

51. If you pretended you were sick to stay home from school, go back to POLICE.

50. THEATRE

Superstars Party

(For super champs of all ages)

THEME: Sports

DRESS: Sport outfits

SETTING: Church hall with table-tennis table

FOOD: Hot-dogs, fruit, biscuits

PURPOSE: To get to know each other's spouses and kids

PROGRAMME: Choose one or two games in each category. Tension breakers for whole group. Team Relays to combine two families OR to divide up families. The BIG Game played with same teams.

EQUIPMENT:

- ☐ Stick-on name tags/felt pens
- ☐ Table-tennis table/bats
- ☐ Game on next page
- ☐ Special equipment for games you choose

Jokes

While everyone is eating, see if someone can guess the answers to these jokes. (Answers on the next page.)

1. What do you get when you put soap suds on the stove?
2. Why did the chicken cross the road?
3. A line of rabbits was crossing the field. They all took one hop backward. What is this called?
4. What's black and white and red all over?
5. What did the big balloon say to the little balloon?
6. What was the elephant doing on the highway?
7. Why did the farmer go over his field with a steam roller?
8. What did the goat say as he ate a reel of film?
9. What happens to frogs when they double park?
10. What's worse than a giraffe with a sore throat?

Tension Breakers

To break the ice and get everyone (especially the kids and spouses) acquainted, here are three tension breakers. Choose one or two and collect the necessary equipment.

DISNEY CHARACTER NAME GUESS

Equipment: Individual stick-on name tags with the names of Disney characters or other characters out of children's literature, such as those given below.

To begin, stick on the back of everyone a different Disney character. The object of the game is to try to guess what Disney character you have on your back. You do this by asking questions from others in the room that can be answered "yes" or "no." For instance, "Is my character an animal?"

On the word GO, everyone mills around, asking questions of others in the room. You can ask only ONE question of a person before going to another person. (The person you ask should also have the chance to ask you one question about their character.) After the exchange, each person moves on to ask a question of another person.

Here are some possible names: ☐ Dumbo ☐ Tigger ☐ Bambi ☐ Peter Pan ☐ Pluto ☐ Jiminy Cricket ☐ Anastasia ☐ Goofy ☐ Captain Hook ☐ Love Bug ☐ Sleeping Beauty ☐ Piglet ☐ Christopher Robin ☐ Prince Charming ☐ Winnie the Pooh ☐ Pinocchio ☐ Thumper ☐ Eyore ☐ Fairy Godmother ☐ Cinderella ☐ Snow White ☐ Dr. Doolittle ☐ Kermit the Frog ☐ Miss Piggy ☐ Paddington ☐ Garfield ☐ Mickey Mouse ☐ Snoopy ☐ Bashful ☐ The Cat In the Hat ☐ Pink Panther ☐ Oscar ☐ Captain Kangeroo ☐ Mister Rogers ☐ Mister Greenjeans.

ROUND THE TABLE

Equipment: Table-tennis table and two bats.

One person picks up a bat at each end of the table. Other players line up behind these two facing clockwise around the table. One person serves, drops bat on table, and moves around the table clockwise as next person picks up bat and prepares to return ball. Continue rotating until someone misses. Player missing drops out of game. When only two are left, players drop bat and turn around once on the spot after hitting the ball and before hitting it the second time. It is considered illegal to hit the ball hard.

PASS THE BALLOON

Equipment: A whistle and two or three large inflated balloons.

Sit in a large circle. Space the balloons around the circle—one balloon every five or six people. When the whistle blows, start passing the balloon around the group. When the whistle blows again, whoever is holding the balloon gets a penalty:

- ☐ First penalty: you must stand up and sit down before you can pass the balloon.
- ☐ Second penalty: you must stand up and turn around before you can pass the balloon.
- ☐ Third penalty: you must stand up, turn around, laugh like a hyena, flap your arms like a bird, and sit down before you can pass the balloon.

Remember, when the whistle blows, start passing balloons to the right. When you hear the whistle a second time, the person holding a balloon is penalised. Keep track of your own penalties. (Leader: demonstrate the three penalties.)

Team Relays

Make equal teams by putting two families together or reassigning everyone. Teams should be 6 to 8 people each, including children.

BALANCE THE EGG

Equipment: For each team, one spoon and one hard-boiled egg.

Don't tell anyone that the eggs are hard-boiled. Ask the teams to line up behind the starting line. The first person on each team is given a spoon with an egg on it. On the word GO, the first person on each team runs to the other end of the room and back to the starting line. Then, the next person, etc. The team that finishes first wins.

WATER BALLOON OVER AND UNDER

Equipment: For each team, a strong rubber balloon half filled with water. Have several extra balloons ready in case a balloon pops.

Form each team in a line. Give the first person in each team the balloon. At the word GO, this person passes the balloon over the top of his/her legs to the next person. The second person passes the balloon under his/her legs to the third person. The third person . . . over the head, etc.

When the last person in the line gets the balloon, this person rushes to the front of the line and passes the balloon over his/her head, etc. Continue until the first person on each team comes to the front again.

If a balloon bursts, supply the team with another balloon where it burst.

TABLE-TENNIS FOOTBALL

Equipment: A table-tennis table decorated like a football pitch. Use masking tape for the lines. For goalposts, straws stuck in blue-tack with the crossbar fastened with pins.

Each team sits alternately around the table. The middle person at each end of the table (goal) is on the offensive, while the two on the outside are defensive.

With a table-tennis ball on the centre-spot, the referee blows the whistle. Everyone, with hands under the table, and chin on the table, blows the ball toward the opponent's goal. If the ball falls off the table, place it where it fell off and continue. Score 6 points for every goal.

Throw-ins, corners, and cheering sections enhance the enthusiasm. Team with most points wins. Vary the rules and game for your situation.

Answers to Jokes
1. Foam on the range.
2. To see a man laying bricks.
3. A receding hare line.
4. A chocolate sundae covered with ketchup.
5. My pop is bigger than your pop.
6. About two miles an hour.
7. He wanted to raise mashed potatoes.
8. "I liked the book better."
9. They get toad away.
10. A hippopotamus with chapped lips.

The BIG Game *(Next Page)*

Equipment: One game (on next page), score pad, and score keeper.
1. Divide into two teams. Young kids divided equally between the teams.
2. Referee reads the first question. The YOUNGEST person on Team A gets first try. If this person does not know the answer, the YOUNGEST person on Team B gets a try. If neither of these answers correctly, the question goes to the NEXT YOUNGEST, etc., until someone answers correctly.
3. Scoring is based on the age of the person who answers correctly:
   ☐ Ages 4 to 10, a correct answer = 10 points
   ☐ Ages 11 to 12, a correct answer = 8 points
   ☐ Ages 13 to 14, a correct answer = 6 points
   ☐ Ages 15 to 90, a correct answer = 4 points
4. When a team scores, the next question goes to the other team first.
5. On EXTRA POINTS, the ages are reversed. The OLDEST person on the team gets the first chance; then the next oldest, etc.
6. Scoring for EXTRA POINTS is based on the ages:
   ☐ Ages 15 to 90, a correct answer = 3 points
   ☐ Ages 12 to 14, a correct answer = 2 points
   ☐ Ages 4 to 11, a correct answer = 1 point.

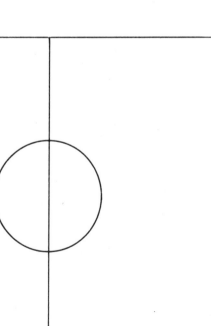

OUR COUNTRY

FACTS: What is the . . .
1. Capital
2. National anthem
3. Flag
4. Patron Saint's Day
5. Longest river
6. Highest mountain
7. Largest county
8. Second city
9. Tallest building
10. Nearest place to France

FAMOUS PLACES: Where is . . .
1. Buckingham Palace
2. Mersey Tunnel
3. Conway Castle
4. Princes Street
5. Stormont
6. Stonehenge
7. Clifton Suspension Bridge
8. Ambridge
9. Hampton Court
10. Ilkley Moor

FAMOUS PEOPLE: Who is associated with . . .
1. Nursing and a lamp
2. Abolition of slavery
3. Invention of TV
4. First railway
5. Votes for women
6. Discovery of Australia
7. Founding the Scouts
8. Stratford-upon-Avon
9. Sherwood Forest
10. Gunpowder Plot

EXTRA POINTS: (for the older people in the group to guess)
1. Who won the F.A. Cup this year?
2. Who got a knighthood this year?
3. Which is the top-selling car?
4. Who are the Test Matches against this year?
5. Who won the Boat Race?
6. When is the next Motor Show?
7. Who won the Eurovision Song Contest?
8. Who is the TV Personality of the Year?
9. Who is the Wimbledon Ladies Singles Champion?
10. Who is Mr. Speaker?

OUR TOWN

FACTS: What is the . . .
1. Origin of the name
2. Tallest building
3. Closest library
4. Largest park
5. Early closing day
6. Nearest fire station
7. Thing that your town is famous for
8. Local newspaper
9. Local Council
10. Favourite place with teenagers

HISTORIC PLACES: Where is the . . .
1. Oldest building still standing
2. War memorial
3. Oldest house
4. Oldest church
5. Original police station
6. Oldest school
7. Oldest grave
8. Oldest shop
9. Museum
10. Registrar's Office

FAMOUS PEOPLE: Who is the . . .
1. Mayor
2. Newspaper editor
3. M.P.
4. Most famous resident
5. Chairman of the Council
6. Football club manager
7. Soapbox orator on local issues
8. Most colourful citizen
9. Most outstanding teacher
10. Strong moral influence

EXTRA POINTS: (For the older people to answer)
1. What is the most picturesque spot in the town?
2. What is the most appealing thing about the town?
3. Where is your favourite eating spot?
4. Where would you go for a romantic evening?
5. Which local newspaper do you read most?
6. Who is your choice for your most unforgettable character?
7. In planning a tour of your community, where would you start?
8. What spot would you say was the most historic?
9. Who do the teenagers in your town look to for values?
10. Who would you nominate in your town as the Citizen of the Year?

OUR CHURCH

FACTS: What is our church . . .
1. Minister's full name
2. Denomination
3. Hymn book
4. Founder (human)
5. Type of government
6. Style of architecture
7. National headquarters
8. Origin of our name
9. Oldest part of building
10. Version of Bible used most

MEMORIES: Share the first time you remember . . .
1. Coming to your church
2. Feeling really accepted
3. Favourite Sunday school teacher
4. Turning over your life to God
5. Getting into Scripture
6. Belonging to a close group
7. Going on a trip/retreat
8. Favourite thing about church
9. About your group at church
10. About God himself

FAMOUS PEOPLE: Who in your church . . .
1. Snores during the sermon
2. Looks like Mr. Universe
3. Reminds you of Charlie Brown
4. The most colourful character
5. Best comedian
6. Is fun to be around
7. Makes people feel warm
8. The jogger
9. Like Mister Rogers
10. The bionic woman

EXTRA POINTS:
1. Would your minister be more like Robin Day or Terry Wogan?
2. Would your youth leader be more like Morecombe or Wise?
3. Would your church programme be more like Chitty, Chitty Bang, Bang or Porsche Turbo Carraro?
4. What is very special about your church?
5. What are you most proud of about your church?
6. What would you miss if you had to move?
7. Where has your church improved in the last year?
8. What is your biggest hope for your church?

Family Reunion Party

(After an old-fashioned family picnic)

THEME: The "good old" days.

DRESS: The oldest clothes you have

SETTING: Indoors and outdoors for different games

FOOD: An "old-fashioned" church picnic basket—sandwiches, crisps, cakes, pop.

PURPOSE: To get to know each other's spouses and kids.

PROGRAMME: Choose one or two games in each category. Tension breakers for whole group. Team Games to combine two or more families who will stay together for the Big Game at the close.

EQUIPMENT:

☐ Large, soft ball

☐ Stick-on-name tags/felt pens

☐ Pencil and paper for everyone

Jokes

While everyone is eating, see if anyone can guess the answers to these jokes. (Answers on the next page.)

1. What has two legs but can't walk?
2. What did Napoleon do with his armies?
3. What do you get when you cross a jelly with a sheep-dog?
4. How do you get down off an elephant?
5. What is an octopus?
6. Why did the watch stop working?
7. Why did the boy throw butter out the window?
8. What's black and white and blue all over?
9. What is a caterpillar?
10. How do you make a hamburger stand?

Tension Breakers

To break the ice and get everyone (especially the kids and spouses) acquainted, here are three tension breakers. Choose one or two and collect the necessary equipment.

ADVERTISING SLOGANS

Equipment: A pencil and sheet of paper for everyone.

Beforehand think of twenty well-known (and some old-fashioned) slogans that have been used to promote products. Give out a pencil and paper to everyone. Ask the people in silence to jot down the *product* or finish the slogan. Read the slogan . . . leaving off the name or product . . . and pause for everyone to jot down the product on their sheet of paper. When you are finished, go over the slogans and have everyone grade their paper. The person with the most correct answers WINS. Here are a few to start with. Add some

new ones and some very old ones.

☐ Things go better with (Coke) ☐ Everything you want and a little bit more (Safeway) ☐ When you care enough to send the very best (Hallmark) ☐ Put a tiger in your tank (Esso) ☐ We try harder (Avis) ☐ Make someone happy (British Telecom) ☐ We'll take more care of you (British Airways) ☐ The caring, sharing . . . (Co-op) ☐ We never forget you have a choice (British Caledonian) ☐ Trusted for two centuries (Phoenix Assurance) ☐ Enter a different world (Harrods) ☐ So much more to value (Boots) ☐ Better. By Design. (Vauxhall)

BEAN BLITZ

Equipment: An envelope with twenty beans for each person.

Give an envelope with 20 beans in it to each person. Ask people to circulate around the room offering to someone else (one at a time) the chance to guess the number of beans in your closed hand. You can put as many or as few beans in your hand as you wish. You say to the person you approach "Odd or Even." If the person guesses correctly, this person gets the beans. If this person guesses incorrectly, this person must give you the same number of beans in your hand. A time limit is set— 5 minutes—and the person with the most beans at the end wins. When your beans are all gone, you are out.

SHUFFLE YOUR BUNS

Arrange chairs in a circle so each person has a chair. There should be two extra chairs in the circle. Each person sits in a chair except for two people in the middle who try to sit in the two vacant chairs. The people sitting on the chairs keep moving around from chair to chair to prevent the two in the middle from sitting down. If one or both of the two in the middle manage to sit in a chair, the person on their right replaces them in the middle of the circle and then tries to sit in an empty chair.

Team Games

When you split into teams for these games, **keep the families together on the same teams** so that they will be together for the BIG Game later on. One team could have two families as long as the team does not add up to more than 8 or 9 people.

HUNGARIAN BASEBALL

Equipment: One soft soccer ball or volley ball.

This game is played like rounders but with these changes. (1) Ball is kicked rather than hit with a bat. (2) When the ball is kicked by the first one in, the entire batting side forms a conga (with hands on waist) and runs around the bowler and back to the batsman's position. (3) The team that is fielding

must retrieve the ball, line up behind the bowler, and pass the ball back to him *under their legs.* The team that completes the process first either scores a point or gets someone out. Three outs and side is out. No-balls don't count.

COMMUNICATION

Equipment: Sealed envelopes with identical telegram type messages in the envelopes for each team.

This is the old game of "gossip" with a twist. Each team is split in half—half going to the other end of the room and half staying behind the starting line. On the word GO, one person from each team is given a sealed envelope with a rather complicated message in it. This person opens the envelope, reads the message, tears it up, and throws it away. This person then *runs* to the next person (opposite end of room) and whispers the message. Then the second person runs back to the next person and whispers the message . . . and so on until the last person runs to the supervisor and whispers it to him. The team closest to the original message wins. Accuracy, not time, is the crucial factor.

SCAVENGER HUNT

Equipment: Whatever is in your wallet, purse or pockets.

This game is played like an "old-fashioned" scavenger hunt, except this time the teams have to produce the items from things they have in their possession.

One person acts as the referee in the centre of the room. Each team sits in a cluster, equidistant from the referee in the centre. The referee calls out an item, such as a shoelace . . . and the first team to bring this item to the referee in the centre of the room is the winner. Points are awarded to the team based on the "difficulty factor" in obtaining the items. The referee keeps score and periodically announces the score. (If one team is ahead, the referee can equalize the score by awarding a few extra points for the next item.)

Here is a list of items and suggested points. Call out one item at a time. For 100 points, the first team to bring to the referee a:

☐ sock with a hole in it
☐ picture of the Queen (on a coin)
☐ something that smells   ☐ baby picture
☐ picture of the Duke of Wellington (£5 note)
☐ used ticket   ☐ love letter
☐ 50 cent coin   ☐ dirty comb

For 200 points, the first team to bring to the referee:

☐ eight shoelaces tied end to end
☐ three shirts on one person backwards and buttoned up
☐ 89p in change
☐ three different coloured hairs tied together
☐ four shoes that total 29 in shoe sizes . . . tied together

For 300 points, the first team to bring to the referee:

☐ two people inside one shirt . . . all buttoned up
☐ one person with 4 belts, 3 shirts, and 8 socks on
☐ first team to line up in a row according to shoe size

For 500 points, the first team to bring to the referee:

☐ the whole team surrounded by a rope made out of socks

The BIG Game

Equipment: Score card and pencil for each game.

This is a game that could last all night . . . and all the next week if you wanted it to. In fact, it would be a good supper table game for families to take home with them. The object of the game is to find out how much the kids know about their mums and dads, grandparents and family history.

To make the game more exciting for the kids, you can award points to the family or person that answers correctly, based on the age of the person.

☐ 10 points if the person is under age six
☐ 8 points if the person is between age 6 and 8
☐ 6 points if the person is between age 9 and 11
☐ 4 points if the person is between age 12 and 14
☐ 2 points if the person is over 14.

At the party, two or more families should compete against each other, like a typical TV quiz show. One family goes first on ROUND ONE. One of the parents reads the questions and the kids answer. (Obviously, the younger kid should try to answer first because you get more points.)

Then, move to the next family and have one of the parents read the same questions and have their kids answer . . . etc., until one parent in each family has read the questions on ROUND ONE. Then, go around (if you have time) and have the other parent in each family read the questions . . . or move on to ROUND TWO.

If you keep the whole group together (with all the families), you will only have time for ROUND ONE . . . and this is fine. The important thing is to have fun with your kids—letting your kids guess about their parents. TAKE TIME TO TELL THE "STORIES" OF YOUR CHILDHOOD, HARD TIMES, BEAUTIFUL MEMORIES, AND FAMILY TRADITIONS THAT YOUR KIDS NEED TO HEAR.

Answers to Jokes
1. A pair of pants.
2. Put them in his sleevies.
3. Collie-wobbles.
4. You don't. You get down off ducks.
5. An eight-sided cat.
6. It ran out of time.
7. He wanted to see the butterfly.
8. A zebra in a snowstorm.
9. An upholstered worm.
10. Take away its chair.

Mum and Dad's Childhood

1. Where was I born?
2. Was I born at home or in a hospital?
3. Was I bottle-fed or breast-fed as a baby?
4. Who was I named after?
5. Who read to me at night or heard my prayers?
6. Who did I go to for sympathy when I was hurt?
7. Who was the disciplinarian in my family?
8. Who was my favourite uncle or aunt?
9. What food did I hate to eat?
10. What was my favourite pet?
11. What was my favourite game before the age of 10?
12. What was my favourite pastime as a child?
13. What was my favourite toy as a child?
14. Did I belong to any club like Scouts?
15. When did I learn how to swim?
16. What did I want to be when I grew up?

Mum and Dad's School Days

1. Where was I living when I started primary school?
2. How did I get to school?
3. What subject in primary school was I best in?
4. What subject in primary school gave me the most trouble?
5. Who helped me with my homework?
6. Who was my favourite author or what was my favourite kind of literature?
7. What was my favourite sport when I was a kid?
8. Where in my house did I do my homework?
9. Did I ever play truant from school?
10. Was I ever sent to the headmaster's office?
11. What was my favourite subject in secondary school?
12. What exam did I fail?
13. How did I spend my summer holidays?
14. What was my first paying job?
15. What was my favourite music when I was a teenager?
16. What was my favourite pastime when I was a teenager?

Mum and Dad's Home Life

1. What kind of house did I live in when I was a child?
2. How did we heat our house when I was a child?
3. Did I crawl in bed with my parents when I was a child?
4. What chore did I hate to do?
5. Did I keep my room very tidy?
6. Did I share my bedroom with anyone else?
7. What was the fun thing we did a lot as a family?
8. Did I participate in any team games?
9. Did my parents come to the games when I was playing?
10. Was I ever on a championship team?
11. Who usually waited up for me when I was out late?
12. What was my mother's favourite food?
13. What was my father's favourite pastime?
14. Who tried to tell me about "the birds and the bees"?
15. How old was I when I got kissed for the first time outside my family?
16. Who in my family was the nuisance or mischief-maker when I was courting?

Mum and Dad's Parents and Relatives

1. Where was my father born?
2. Where was my mother born?
3. Where did my father spend most of his childhood?
4. Where did my mother spend most of her childhood?
5. When did my father leave school?
6. When did my mother leave school?
7. What was my father doing when he met my mother?
8. Where did my parents get married?
9. Where did my parents live right after they got married?
10. What was my father's occupation?
11. Who was the big "story teller" among our family relations?
12. Who was the practical joker in my family relations?
13. Who was the tower of strength in times of family crisis?
14. Who would come the closest to being the "colourful character" in my family?
15. What is the outstanding strength in my father?
16. What is the outstanding strength in my mother?

A '60's Party

(with prize for the most authentic '60's Flower Power outfit)

THEME: the '60's

DRESS: Like teenagers dressed in the '60's

SETTING: Indoors except for one optional game

FOOD: Fish and chips

PURPOSE: To get to know each other's spouses and kids

PROGRAMME: Choose one or two games in each category. Tension breakers for whole group. Team Games to combine two or more families or split up families. The teams will stay together for the BIG Game at the close.

EQUIPMENT:

☐ Stick-on name tags/felt pens

☐ Large balloons

☐ Game "Tell Us About" on page 142 for each team, plus one dice or spinner for each game

Jokes

While everyone is eating, see if someone can guess the answers to these jokes. (Answers on the next page.)

1. What do you get when you cross a refrigerator and a stereo?
2. What do you do when you break your toe?
3. What's a frog's favourite sweet?
4. How do you know if an elephant has been in your refrigerator?
5. What's red and goes beep, beep?
6. Why did the chicken cross the road?
7. What's black and white and red all over?
8. Why can't a nose be twelve inches long?
9. What's worse than a giraffe with a sore throat?
10. Why did the boy throw a clock out the window?

Tension Breakers

To break the ice and get everyone (especially the kids and spouses) acquainted, here are three tension breakers. Choose one or two and collect the necessary equipment.

PAPER AEROPLANE CONTEST
Equipment: A sheet of paper (for making aeroplanes) for everyone.

Everyone makes their own paper aeroplane. While they are doing this, set up a target on the floor that looks like a dart board with a bull's eye and two outer circles. The bull's eye is worth 20 points. The middle ring, 10 points. And the outside ring, 5 points. Each person gets to throw his/her aeroplane three times. The one with the most points wins.

ALL CHANGE
Equipment: One chair for each person.

Group sits in a circle. Leader calls out a description, say, "Those wearing blue socks." Everyone who fits description must change places with someone. While people are moving around, a chair is removed. The last person with a chair is the winner. Suitable descriptions include: "Those wearing jeans," "Those who use Spray Fresh." "Those who like pickled onions." Every few goes, include one which will make everyone move: "Those with feet," "Those who breathe air," etc.

STAND UP
Equipment: None

Sit in the group with a partner, back to back, feet in front of you, and arms linked. Then, try to stand up *together.* After you succeed add another twosome and try again. Keep adding people until your whole group is trying to stand together.

Team Games

Make two equal teams by putting families together or reassigning everyone.

PASS THE FEETBALL

Equipment: A large round inflated balloon for each team, plus a couple of extras in case a balloon pops.

Give each team a large balloon. Blow up the balloon to the size of a watermelon. Each team sits in a circle with feet in the middle. On the word GO, pass the balloon around your team, using only your feet. (If it touches your hands, you have to start over.) The first group to pass the balloon *five* times around WINS.

MOTORBOAT

Equipment: None

Make believe your team is a motor. See how much speed you can achieve. At the word GO, the first person turns their head to the right, giving the sound for the specified motor. Then, the next person turns their head to the right, repeating the sound, etc. The first team to finish the number of laps should clap to signal they have finished.

☐ Round One: Motorboats . . . for five laps . . . and the sound is "putt."

☐ Round Two: Motorcycles . . . for seven laps . . . and the sound is "rrrr."

☐ Round Three: Racing cars at the Indianapolis Speedway . . . for twenty laps . . . and the sound is "zoooooommmmmmmmm."

Leader: Demonstrate these sounds by turning your head quickly to the right and *really* making the sound like the particular motor. On Round Three, ask teams to move in close so that their heads are nearly touching . . . and they are making almost one continuous sound.

Answers to Jokes
1. Cool music.
2. Call a toe truck.
3. A lollihop
4. There are footprints in the peanut butter.
5. A strawberry in a traffic jam.
6. To get to the other side.
7. A newspaper.
8. Then it would be a foot.
9. A centipede with athlete's foot.
10. He wanted to see time fly.

CHARLIE CHAPLIN RELAY

Equipment: Balloon, bag of crisps, cane/walking stick for each team.

Teams line up for a normal relay race, course length 10 yards. Crisps, balloon, and cane are placed in front of each team at start. First player places balloon between his knees, crisps on his head and moves along course as fast as possible, whilst twirling cane, Charlie Chaplin style. He then passes balloon, crisps, and cane to next player on his team. If he drops the crisps or balloon, they must be replaced before he moves on. First team to complete course wins. Have plenty of spare balloons available for when they burst.

FLAMINGO FOOTBALL

Equipment: Football and large garden/field.

Announce that you are going to play football. The rules are the same except for this one exception. All the men over 12 must hold their left foot with their right hand at all times. They must run, pass, even kick, all on one foot. Play for 4 periods of 2 minutes each.

GUESS WHO

Equipment: A set of stick-on name tags with famous people or characters in the movies or comics on these name tags, such as: ☐ Liberace ☐ Miss Piggy ☐ Romeo and Juliet ☐ E.T. ☐ Manchester United ☐ Lady Godiva ☐ John Denver ☐ Cliff Richard ☐ Your minister ☐ A local celebrity ☐ The latest teenage pop star ☐ Three little pigs ☐ Kermit the Frog.

While the Leader is explaining the directions, have two helpers go to each team and put a *different* stick-on name tag on the back of *each* person on the team.

On the word GO, one person in each team turns around and lets the others on the team see the name tag on his/her back. Then, the others start acting out (in silence) this character until the person can guess who it is. The second person on the team turns around and lets the others see the name tag. The others act out this character until the person can guess who it is, etc., until everyone on the team has guessed their name tag. The first team to complete the process WINS.

BUZZ-FIZZ

Equipment: None

Sit with your team in a circle. Try to count up to 50 as fast as you can, but instead of saying "five" or any multiple of "five," say "BUZZ." Instead of saying "seven" or any multiple of "seven," say "FIZZ."

For example, each person, in turn around your team, will sound off with "one," "two," "three," "four," and the next person will say "BUZZ"; the next person "six" and the next person "FIZZ," etc.

If the number is a multiple of "five" and "seven," say "BUZZ-FIZZ." If you make a mistake, start over. The first group to reach 50 WINS.

RHYTHM

Equipment: None

Everyone sits in a circle and numbers off (1, 2, 3, 4, etc.). The number 1 person starts the "rhythm," which is in four steps: (1) slap your thighs, (2) clap, (3) snap your right fingers, and (4) snap your left fingers . . . in a moderately slow rhythm . . . 1-2-3-4-1-2-3-4-1-etc. (It may speed up after everyone learns how to play.)

The real action begins when the number one person, as he/she snaps his/her right fingers, calls out his/her own number (One), and as he/she snaps his/her left fingers, calls out someone else's number. For example, it might sound like this: (slap) (clap) "ONE, SIX," and then the number six person (keeping in the rhythm) might go: (slap) (clap) "SIX, TEN," and then the number ten person would do the same thing, calling out someone else's number on the second finger snap, and so on. If anyone misses, this person goes to the end and everyone who was after this person moves up one number. The object is to eventually arrive at the number one chair.

(Leader: If there are more than 10 or 12, divide into two groups. A good average for this tension breaker is 8 to 10 people in a group.)

The BIG Game

Equipment: The game "Tell Us About" on pages 14-15 for each team, plus one dice or spinner for each game.

Pass out the game to each team. Ask every player to find a mover, such as a penny, a key, etc. . . . and place their mover on START. The game is played exactly like Monopoly. Everyone rolls the dice and advances their mover. This person must "Tell About" whatever they land on.

To reach the Finish, you must roll the exact number.

Hint: For more fun, divide your team into partners and require that everyone on the team must finish before you win.

Quiz Show Party

(To beat anything on TV)

THEME: TV Quiz Show

DRESS: Casual

SETTING: Indoors or outdoors or both

FOOD: Spaghetti

PURPOSE: To get to know each other's spouses and kids

PROGRAMME: Choose one or two games in each category. Tension breakers for the whole group. Team Games to combine two families OR divide up families. The BIG GAME played with the same teams.

EQUIPMENT:

☐ Stick-on name tags/felt pens

☐ Game "Quiz" on pages 10-11 for each team (Photocopy or use book)

☐ Special equipment for each game

Jokes

While everyone is eating, see if someone can guess the answers to these jokes. (Answers on the next page.)

1. What has four wheels and flies?
2. What makes oil boil?
3. What goes ninety-nine bonk?
4. Why did the cow jump over the moon?
5. What did the digital clock say to his mother?
6. Why do leopards never escape from the zoo?
7. What's black and white and red all over?
8. On which side does the chicken have the most feathers?
9. What do you get when your cat eats a lemon?
10. If athletes get athlete's foot, what do astronauts get?

Tension Breakers

To break the ice and get everyone (especially the kids and spouses) acquainted, here are three tension breakers. Choose one or two and collect the necessary equipment.

CIRCLE BALL

Equipment: Whistle and football or large inflated balloon

Everyone sits in a circle. The leader gives the ball to someone in the group.

This is the old game of "hot potato" with a twist. Instead of passing the "hot potato" from person to person around the circle, the "hot potato" is passed FORWARD two people and BACK one person around the circle. For instance, if the person who is holding the ball now is 1, this person would pass the ball FORWARD to 3. Then, 3 would pass the ball BACK to 2. And 2 would pass the ball FORWARD to 4. And 4 would pass the ball BACK to 3, etc. . . . around the circle.

When the whistle blows, start passing the ball. When the whistle blows again, the person with the "hot potato" is OUT. Keep eliminating people until you are down to two. Then, pass the ball back and forth until one of these two is eliminated.

SPUD

Equipment: One football and lots of room.

All players are numbered consecutively. One player throws the ball high in the air and calls a number. Person with that number catches the ball and cries, "Spud." Other players have been running away, but must stop and stand still when catcher cries out. If the person whose number was called can catch the ball before it hits the ground, this person can take three steps toward any other player before throwing the ball. This person then tries to hit someone with the ball. If he/she does, this player receives an "S." If he/she misses, the thrower gets an "S." When a player receives S,P,U,D, this person is OUT.

MATCH GAME

Equipment: The first list to be given to everyone and the articles on the second list placed on a large table.

Distribute the list to everyone, along with a pencil.

1. Doughnut
2. The colonel
3. A famous band
4. Looks like a foot
5. Headquarters
6. A stirring event
7. The end of winter
8. A pair of slippers

9. Sheep container
10. An old beau of mine
11. The peacemaker
12. There love is found
13. Bruise
14. Glass of water
15. A place for reflection
16. The reigning favorite
17. A morning caller
18. Partly open door
19. Sharpens iron
20. Fire when ready
21. Drive through the wood
22. Bound to shine
23. Life of China
24. Top dog
25. My native land

Next, place the articles listed below on a large table or around the room that will match the "clues" given in the first list. For example, the corresponding items for the preceding list would be:
1. The letter "o" on a card
2. Kernel of corn
3. Rubber band
4. Ruler
5. Pillow
6. Spoon
7. Letter "r"
8. Two banana peels
9. Pen
10. Old ribbon bow
11. Pair of scissors
12. Dictionary
13. Two tea bags (brews)
14. Blotter or sponge
15. Mirror
16. Umbrella
17. Alarm clock
18. A jar
19. Electric iron
20. Match
21. Nail
22. Shoe polish
23. Rice
24. Hot dog
25. Dirt

The winner is the person who can correctly match up all the items in the shortest time. To make the game harder, place twice as many items on the table as you have clues for.

Team Games

Make two teams. The teams formed at this time Will stay together for The BIG Game (Quiz) later

on. If you have more than 20, divide into teams of 8 to 10 people each.

BLIND VOLLEYBALL
Equipment: A volleyball and a solid divider that can obstruct the view of the other team, such as blankets hung over a regular volleyball net or rope. (The divider should also be low enough so that players cannot see under it.)

. The game is played exactly like volleyball except for two slight changes: (1) everyone must sit on the floor, and (2) you can hit the ball as many times as you wish before it crosses the "net."

BALLOON POP RELAY
Equipment: large rubber balloons and two chairs.

Place two chairs at end of room with a pile of rubber balloons beside each chair. Teams line up single file behind starting line. On the word GO, first person on each team runs to the chair at the other end of the room, blows up the balloon and sits on it until it pops. Then, this person returns to starting line and tags the next person, etc. . . . until all of the balloons are popped.

DODGE BALL
Equipment: Soft rubber volleyball and plenty of room.

One team forms a circle while the opposing team scatters inside the circle. Players forming the circle throw the ball and attempt to hit the players inside the circle. Players inside the circle may dodge any way they choose, but they cannot leave the circle. A player who is hit is eliminated from the game. Scoring: The time required to eliminate all the players on a team is determined. The team that takes the longest to be eliminated WINS.

Answers to Jokes
1. Dustbin lorry.
2. The letter "b."
3. A centipede with a wooden leg.
4. The farmer's hands were cold.
5. "Look, Ma. No hands."
6. Because they're always spotted.
7. A zebra with sunburn.
8. The outside.
9. A sour puss.
10. Missile-toes.

The BIG Game

Equipment: For each team, the "Quiz" game on pages 10-11, and a pencil and paper scorecard for each person.

This game is played like a TV quiz show, with each person keeping their own score. Points are made by guessing correctly about other people on your team as they read one of the quiz cards on the game.

Ask each team to sit in a circle and hand one game to someone on each team. To begin, the person with the game selects ONE of the cards on the game, such as "Entertainment." This person then reads aloud the 1 point question on this card, such as: "For 1 point I would likely: (a) go out to the cinema, or (b) stay home for a TV rerun."

Then, everyone on the team tries to guess what this person's answer is BEFORE this person explains. All who guessed RIGHT win 1 point each. (Jot down on your scorecard the points you win after each guess.)

Then, the person with the game reads the 2 points question in this category and the others try to guess the answer BEFORE this person explains.

When the first person has read all of the questions in ONE category, he/she passes the game to the next person in the circle. This person, in turn, chooses another card on the game and reads through the questions . . . having team members try to guess the answer BEFORE he/she shares their answer.

When everyone on the team has read a card on the game, the person with the most points WINS.

Hint: To make the game even more fun, divide your team into partners and combine individual scores to determine which partners WIN.

EXTENDED FAMILY SOCIAL 6

Frog Kissing Party

(For frogs that need a kiss)

THEME: Affirmation (Seeing beautiful things in each other)

DRESS: Anything green *and* a hat that fits your personality

SETTING: Indoors / large basement

FOOD: Each family brings a main course and a sweet to be shared

PURPOSE: To affirm and be affirmed by each other, using the story of the frog that became a prince. (See below)

PROGRAMME: Choose one or two tension breakers to start off the evening. Then, read the parable of the frog and spend the rest of the evening playing the affirmation games.

EQUIPMENT

- ☐ Stick-on name tags/felt pens
- ☐ A copy of the "Guess Who" game on pages 24-25 for everyone
- ☐ Large selection of hats
- ☐ Special equipment for each game
- ☐ Piece of paper and pencil for game

Tension Breakers

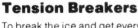

To break the ice and get everyone (especially the kids and spouses) acquainted, here are some tension breakers. Choose one or two and collect the necessary equipment.

MUSICAL HATS

Equipment: A whistle and an old hat for everyone. (Ask everyone to bring a hat—any kind.)

Give a hat to everyone in the room except for one person. Ask each to put on a hat and stand in a circle. This game is played like "musical chairs," but instead of a missing chair, there is a missing hat.

When the whistle blows, everyone starts walking in a circle. With their right hand ONLY, they grab the hat on the head of the person in front of them and place the hat on their own head. When the whistle blows again, the person without a hat on their head is OUT.

The object of the game is to keep a hat on your head by grabbing the hat on the head of the person in front of you and putting it on your head.

You cannot use your left hand to hold your hat on your head. All you can do is take the hat off the head of the person in front of you and put their hat on your head.

Now, get in a circle and turn right. When you hear the whistle, start walking and removing hats. When the whistle blows again, the person without a hat is OUT.

(Leader: Remove a hat after each round . . . until there are only two people left. Ask these two

POEM: This poem is the theme for the evening. Read it aloud at an appropriate time.

Once upon a time . . .
　there was a frog.
But he wasn't *really* a frog.
He was a prince
　who looked and felt like a frog.
A wicked witch had cast a spell on him
　and only the kiss of a beautiful maiden
　　could save him.
But no one wanted to kiss this frog!
So there he sat—an unkissed prince in
　　frog form.
But . . . one day, along came a beautiful
　　maiden
　who gave this frog a great big smack.
　CRASH—BOOM—ZAP!
There he was . . .
　a handsome, dashing prince.
(And you know the rest—they lived
　　happily ever after.)

SO, what is the task of the church?
To kiss frogs, of course!

　　　　　　　　　　—Wes Seeliger

to stand one foot apart and keep swapping the one hat until the whistle blows. Delay the final whistle until the tension really mounts.)

AFFIRMATION HATS

Equipment: A list of make-believe hats below, OR a collection of real hats from your attic—the more the better.

Pass out a sheet of paper with the list of the hats below on it . . . or assemble in the middle of the room a collection of actual hats. Ask everyone IN SILENCE to think about the others in the room and jot down the names of the others (or make a mental note) next to the hat that you would match with their personality. For instance,

you might put Bill's name next to the "Fishing Hat" because you see Bill as homey and comfortable, like an old fishing hat. If you have actual hats to choose from, just make a mental note.

Then, ask one person to sit in silence while the others explain what hat they picked for this person and why. If you are using actual hats, you may want to pick up the hat and go into detail in your "matchmaking."

When you have finished with the first person, ask the next person in the group to sit in silence while the others explain their choice of hat for this person, etc. . . . until you have gone all the way around the group.

(Leader: If you have more than 10 or 12 at the party, you'd better divide into two groups . . . or you will be at this game all evening.)

EASTER HAT: pink and pretty—light and frilly, just right for the parade.
TOP HAT: grand and stately, proper and elegant, fit for the inaugural ball.
FISHING HAT: homey and comfortable, showing the marks of lots of use and of good times out in the open.
COWBOY HAT: designed for the drugstore cowboy to wear when telling about the good ole days when men were men.
MOTORCYCLE HELMET: for cool cats and modern-day adventurers whipping along the open road.
SOMBRERO: for the happy-go-lucky, easy-going romantic who sees life as a song.
COONSKIN CAP: for the spirited pioneer who is always looking for new frontiers.
FUN HAT: childlike, playful, delightfully mischievous.
SAFARI HAT: rugged, designed for the most daring adventurer, lover of danger and challenge.
BOWLER, with umbrella: proper, precise, for the undauntable, in control even if the world falls in.
BEACH HAT: for outdoors, sunny, just right for teasing.
HARD HAT: strong, protective, ready for hazardous missions.
BONNET: sweet and untainted, for the hardworker, holding to what's right.
SANTA CLAUS CAP: for the happy one who loves to give surprises.
TURBAN: silent, mysterious, aloof, yet probably wanting to be known.
CHIFFON VEIL: provocative, alluring and mischievous, for the open-hearted flirt.
Woolly POM-POM HAT: beautifully childlike, good for long walks in the woods and making snowmen.
Artist's BERET: sensitive, a bit rakish, just right for lovers of all ages.
Luminous SPACE HELMET: out-of-this world, just right for the high-flying dreamer.
MORTARBOARD, with tassle: brainy, sophisticated, worn invisibly to the meetings of the Board.
White SAILOR HAT: unpretentious, for the one eager to see the world, at home on sea or land or anywhere.
STRAW HAT and cane: for the showman, gallant and fun-loving.
FLAT CAP: relaxed, light-hearted, for the carefree, some-nonsense, jolly fellow.

AFFIRMATION MUSICAL INSTRUMENTS
Equipment: The list of musical instruments below and a pencil for everyone.
This game is played exactly like the game above.
ANGELIC HARP: soft, gentle, melodious, wooing with heavenly sounds.
OLD-FASHIONED WASHBOARD: authentic, non-conforming, childlike, and fun.
PLAYER PIANO: mischievous, raucous, honky-tonk—delightfully carefree.
KETTLE DRUM: strong, vibrant, commanding when needed but usually in the background.
PASSIONATE CASTANET: with Spanish fervor, stormy, wild, seductive—with rose in mouth.
STRADIVARIUS VIOLIN: priceless, exquisite, soul piercing—with the touch of the master.
FLUTTERING FLUTE: tender, lighthearted, wide-ranging, and clear as crystal.
SCOTTISH BAGPIPES: martial, visceral, moving—distinctive and unmistakable.
SQUARE DANCE FIDDLE: folksy, down-to-earth, toe tapping—sprightly and lighthearted.
ENCHANTING OBOE: haunting, charming, disarming—even the Cobra is harmless with this sound.
MELLOW CELLO: deep, sonorous, compassionate—adding body and depth to the orchestra.
PIPE ORGAN: grand, magnificent, richly endowed—versatile and commanding.
HERALDING TRUMPET: stirring, lively, invigorating—signaling attention and attack.
CLASSICAL GUITAR: thoughtful, contemplative, profoundly entertaining, and entertainingly profound.
ONE-MAN BAND: Harmonica in mouth. Accordion in hands. Noisy drum on rear end.
COMB AND TISSUE PAPER: makeshift, original, uncomplicated—homespun and creative.
SENSUOUS TROMBONE: warm, rich, swinging—great in solo or background support.

The BIG Game

Use the same groups as you used in the Tension Breakers.
Equipment: A copy of this game plus a small slip of paper and a pencil for everyone.

1. Write your name on a slip of paper, fold once, and place the slip in the centre of the group.
2. Stir up the slips of paper. Reach in and draw one slip of paper. DO NOT LET ANYONE KNOW THE NAME YOU HAVE PICKED.
3. For the person you have picked, think of an ANIMAL that best describes this person. (If you wish, look over the animals on the game—top section.)

ROUND ONE:
4. First person: Describe the person you have picked as an ANIMAL and let the others guess who this person is. Simply finish the sentence: "The person I have chosen is like a . . . ."
5. Next person: Explain the person you have picked as an ANIMAL and let the others guess.
6. Continue around your group until everyone has explained the person they have as an animal.

ROUND TWO:
7. Put all slips of paper back into the centre of the group. Stir and pick a new slip of paper.
8. Go around and explain the person you picked as a CAR. ("The person reminds me of . . . .") Then the others try to guess who it is.

ROUND THREE
9. Put all slips of paper back into centre of group. Stir and pick a new name.
10. Go around and explain the person you picked as a BOAT. ("This person reminds me of a . . . .") Let the others guess who it is.

It's a Knockout

THEME: Old-style Sunday school outing

DRESS: Old, casual clothes

SETTING: Outdoors/back yard

FOOD: Barbecue

PURPOSE: To have fun

PROGRAMME: The whole evening is built around a medley of relay races. Choose as many or as few as you wish. There is no sequence.

EQUIPMENT:

☐ Stick-on name tags/felt pens

☐ Special equipment for each relay

Team Relays

Divide up the group equally by combining families or reassigning everyone. If you have more than 20, make teams of 8 to 10 people each. Some relays will require the whole team to participate. Some relays need only one or two people from each team, like a track meet. For fun, assign points to the winner of each relay, but keep all the teams in the track meet by juggling the scores.

JUNIOR OLYMPICS (For the kids on each team)
Equipment: paper plate, plastic straw, 4 potato sacks and 4 toilet paper tubes.

Here are some relays that the kids can do well. Ask the captain of each team to pick a contender or relay group for each event.

☐ Discus throw (paper plate)
☐ Javelin (plastic straw)
☐ 100 foot crab crawl (backward)
☐ Potato sack hop relay (4 on each team carrying baton (toilet paper tube) in mouth
☐ Three legged race (two people with one leg each in the potato sack)
☐ Piggyback relay (4 on each team)
☐ Wheelbarrow race relay (4 on each team)

ONE LEGGED BUMPS
Equipment: Circle made with a rope.

Pick two or three men from each team. Stand in the circle, holding your right leg with your left hand. At the signal, participants try to bump each other out of the circle with your body (not with your free hand). Winner is the last one in the circle.

LEAP FROG RELAY
Equipment: Starting line and finish line made out of a rope.

Choose 4 people from each team. Line up behind starting line. On the word GO, first person leans over. Second person leapfrogs over first person and leans over. Third person leapfrogs over first two people and leans over. Fourth person leapfrogs over first three people and leans over. Then, first person leapfrogs over the other three, etc. . . . until you reach the finish line.

STAND OFF
Equipment: Rope for dividing line.

Each team enters two men. Men stand face to face, one arm's length apart, with palms together. The point is to get your opponent off balance, while making contact only with your palms. Each player's feet must be kept together. If your opponent moves his feet, you win. If you both move your feet, do it again. Winners then play each other until you have a champion.

FEETBALL RELAY
Equipment: Tennis ball for each team.

Each team sits in a circle. Captain of each team is given a tennis ball which he puts between his feet. On the word GO, Captains pass the ball to the next person by placing his feet over their feet and letting the ball slip between their feet. Continue passing the ball down the line . . . and back to declare a winner. If you drop the ball, start where the ball was dropped.

SQUARE RELAY

Equipment: Bean bag or balloon for each team.

Each team sits in a line (or kneels on one knee) facing a chair in the middle. (See diagram.) If you have only two teams, line up facing each other. (The circled dot in the diagram is the Captain of each team.)

At the signal, the Captain of each team runs around the chair in the middle and on to the last chair on their side. (Follow on the diagram the route of A.) The last chair is vacant because as soon as the Captain left his place, everybody on the team slid up one chair. Thus number two is now number one.

As soon as the Captain reaches the end chair, this person passes the balloon down the line to the new number one person. This person, in turn, runs around the chair and on to the last chair . . . while everyone on the team is sliding up again . . . and passes the balloon down the line to the new number one person, etc. . . . until the Captain of the team has rotated back to number one chair and receives the balloon.

The first team to complete the rotation and return the balloon to the Captain is the winner.

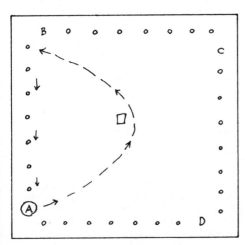

CRAZY RELAY

Equipment: A paper sack for each team with crazy messages inside the sacks.

This is a different kind of relay in which each contestant does something different. What the contestants do is determined by the directions in a bag at the other end of the relay course.

At the beginning of the relay, each team lines up single file as usual. On a signal, the first person on each team runs to the other end of the course and takes a message out of the paper sack, reads it, and proceeds to do what the message requires. Then, this person returns to the starting line and tags the next person. The first team to complete the messages wins. Here are some possible messages for the paper sacks.

1. Run around the chair 5 times while continuously yelling, "The British are coming, the British are coming."

2. Take your shoes off. Put them on the opposite feet, and tag your nearest opponent.

3. Sit on the floor, cross your legs, and sing the following: "Mary had a little lamb, little lamb, little lamb. Mary had a little lamb, its fleece was white as snow."

4. Sit down. Fold your arms, and laugh hard and loud for 5 seconds.

Think up some appropriate messages for the people in your group.

WATER BALLOON TOSS

Equipment: Large rubber balloons filled with water, and rope for dividing line.

Within each team, pair off and stand facing each other across from the dividing line (rope). Each pair is given one balloon filled with water. On the word GO, the person with the balloon tosses the balloon to their partner. If the balloon pops, both are eliminated. If the balloon does not pop, the Leader will ask everyone to take one step backward and prepare for the next toss.

When everyone is in position, the persons with the balloons toss the balloon to their partners. If the balloon does not pop, take one step backwards and prepare for the next round.

Continue tossing the balloons back and forth until only one couple remains.

STOP BALL

Equipment: One soft rubber volley or soccer ball

Organise two teams with not over 10 players on each team. The fielding side scatters over the playing area, while the batting side lines up in single file. The bowler lobs the ball to the first person lined up. This person hits the ball with their fist and runs around their teammates who remain in single file. The fielding team scurries to line up in single file behind whoever succeeds in retrieving the ball.

When the fielding team is lined up behind this person, the ball is passed overhead, from the first player to the last, each player handling the ball in turn.

When the ball reaches the last person in line, all yell "STOP." The batter stops running around his team and counts the number of times he has circled his teammates. This is the score for the inning. The other team now comes up to bat.

After 5 innings, the team with the highest score is the winner.

FULL DRESS

Equipment: Overcoat, gloves, scarf, shoes for each team.

Place the "change of clothes" about 20 feet away from the starting line. Four members from each team are entered in this relay race. On the word GO the first person from each team runs to their clothes, puts them on, runs back to the starting line and takes them off. The next person puts on the clothes, runs to the other end, and takes them off. The third person (like the first person) runs to the other end where the clothes are, puts them on, runs to the starting line, and takes them off. The fourth person, in turn, puts on the clothes, runs to the other end, takes them off, and brings them to the starting line.

Be sure you have clothes that are extra large. 93

Going Away Party

(For saying "Bon Voyage" in fun ways)

THEME: Bon Voyage

DRESS: Your party clothes

SETTING: Indoors and outdoors for different games

FOOD: Buffet

PURPOSE: To say goodbye to the extended family that has been together. The games flow from light, fun, celebrative times to quite serious, deep "gift-giving" at the close. Be sure to save time at the close for deeper sharing.

PROGRAMME: Because this is planned as the last in a series of parties for an extended family of kids and spouses who have been together for several occasions, the selection of games is more purposeful—to set the stage for a "deeper sharing" experience at the close. During the deeper sharing times, provide an alternative for the young kids (even TV) so that the rest of the group can get into the Giving Game without interruption.

EQUIPMENT:

- ☐ Stick-on name tags/felt pens
- ☐ Bon Voyage decorations
- ☐ Four or five large containers of Plasticene
- ☐ Special equipment for all games

Tension Breakers

INSTANT TRAVEL POSTERS
Equipment: A large pile of old magazines— preferably travel brochures—plus a sheet of poster paper for everyone. Also, a few jars of glue or rubber cement.

Everyone is given a chance to make their "dream holiday" travel poster out of tear-outs from old magazines, with pictures, words, slogans, etc., that express what you would like to do and where you would like to go on a "dream holiday."

Give everyone a sheet of poster paper and put

a pile of old magazines in the middle of the circle. Ask everyone to quickly leaf through the magazines, tear out any pictures that strike them, and paste them on the poster with glue.

After 20 minutes, ask everyone to put their poster on the wall with Blue-tack . . . or on the clothes line with clothes pegs.

CONCENTRATION
Equipment: Twenty small household objects on a tray that you might need on a long trip, such as finger nail file, flashlight, small scissors, eyebrow brush, toothbrush, etc. Include some ridiculous things too, like toilet paper.

When you are ready to play the game, uncover the tray in front of the group. Give everyone 2 minutes to memorize what is on the tray. Then, take it away and pass out paper and pencils. Everyone will have 3 minutes in silence to jot down everything they remember. Then, bring the tray back and let everyone check their list. The person with the most correct objects wins.

MOON BALL
Equipment: A very large beach ball—four feet across.

Divide the group into two teams. Establish two goals and start in the middle. The team that can get the ball across the other team's goal WINS.

COORDINATED JUMP
Equipment: Skipping rope with a rag tied on one end . . . or an imaginary rope is okay.

This is "skipping rope" . . . group style. Have the entire group get in a circle, arms over the

shoulders of each other. On the word GO, see if everyone can jump (feet off the floor) at the same instant.

Once you have mastered this, try jumping with an imaginary rope . . . which a person in the middle of the group swings by slowly spinning a pointer around the group. Then, reverse . . . and reverse again.

If you want to use an actual rope, this is okay too.

WATER BALLOON RUGBY
Equipment: 20 large rubber balloons filled with water.

This is touch rugby with a new twist. Instead of using a rugby ball, you will have balloons filled with water.

Normal touch rugby rules apply. Play stops when a player is "tagged" or when a balloon bursts. Have plenty of balloons filled with water ready to put a new balloon into play when one bursts. Have a narrow pitch to force people into passing.

Affirmation Games

These games are designed to allow the group to reflect on their experience together and say "thanks" in fun ways. If you have more than 12 at the party, you'd better split up the group into smaller clusters of 6 to 8 for these games. You should keep people together who know one another. For the small children, let them do something else during this time.

ACADEMY AWARDS

Equipment: A list of Academy Awards and a pencil for everyone. Add to this list some of your own ideas.

It's time for nominations for Academy Awards in your group. Take a few minutes and list the names of the others in your group next to the award you would like to nominate each person for ... one award for each person.

Then, ask one person in each group to sit in silence while the others explain what they have nominated this person for and why. Then, ask the next person to sit in silence and go around a second time ... etc., until you have covered everyone in your group.

_____ ROYAL GIRDLE: for the person who drew us together

_____ MEGAPHONE: for the person who cheered us on

_____ DEAR MARJE AWARD: for the person who patiently listened to our problems

_____ NOBEL PEACE PRIZE: for the person who harmonized our differences

_____ PINK HEART: for the biggest lover in the group

_____ GOLDEN HELMET: for the person who called forth the best in us

_____ SPARK PLUG: for the person who ignited us

_____ PHILLOSAN GUSTO AWARD: for the person who brought lots of gusto

_____ ANDREX TOILET ROLL AWARD: for the person with the soft, tender heart

_____ DAMART THERMAL UNDERWEAR AWARD: for the person who gave us that warm feeling

_____ OLD SPICE AWARD: for the person with the dry wit

_____ ROLLS ROYCE AWARD: for the person who brought the touch of class

_____ THE SERENDIPITY CROWN: for the person I discovered to be the "big" surprise

_____ BIG SHOULDER: for the person who shared our hurts and pain

_____ WALKING STICK: for the person who became a great support to me

DREAM HOMES

Equipment: The list of dream homes for everyone and a pencil.

This is the opposite game from the Academy Awards. This time, you pick your own "special" dwelling that would be appropriate because of what the others in the group have meant to you.

In silence, look over the list and check the "dream home" that fits the NEW you.

_____ SLEEPING BAG: Because you have helped me to get back to simple things, a simple lifestyle—wide open to the outdoors, the stars, smelling flowers, and listening to the birds again.

_____ GLASS HOUSE: Because you have let me be open and free—to look out at the world around, get rid of my rocks, and enjoy life—to let the sun shine in.

_____ MEDIAEVAL CASTLE: Because you have helped me to dream again—of noble causes, chivalry, honor, and valor—even take on the dragons.

_____ SWISS FAMILY TREE HOUSE: Because you have helped me to rebuild my family, work together, see the inner strength in the others, and accept the situation as a new challenge.

_____ CHELSEA APARTMENT: Because you have helped me to know myself, be myself, celebrate the "wild, way-out" side of me as a gift of God, to care less about conformity and "measuring up" to other's expectations.

_____ LOG CABIN: Because you have affirmed my pioneering spirit that strikes out into unknown expeditions, "homesteading" new frontiers in my spiritual journey.

_____ STATELY HOME: Because you have helped me to accept gracious living, culture, relaxing with a mint julip while at the same time calling forth the rebel spirit within me.

_____ VOLKSWAGEN CARAVETTE: Because you have released in me a desire to travel the "back roads" and rediscover my heritage—the old watering places of my childhood and the simple joys of life.

_____ EIGHT-PERSON TENT: Because I want to share more of my life with the rest of you. We have become a family together, and there is so much more we can share.

_____ HOUSEBOAT: Because you have started me on a life cruise into new uncharted waters and new adventures ... and I would like you to share the adventure with me. The pace will be slower and the facilities a little crowded, but you are all welcome.

_____ PORTABLE SANDPIT: Because you have helped me to discover a child inside that I didn't know was there, and the party is just beginning.

_____ TRAVELLING CIRCUS TRAIN: Because you have said it was okay to laugh in the midst of pain, rejoice when times were tough, and celebrate life in all its fullness.

GIVING GAME

Equipment: Anything in your pockets, wallet, or purse. For people who do not have a wallet with them, PROVIDE Plasticene as an option for making gifts.

This game is like a giant Christmas Party, where you exchange gifts with one another. The gifts should somehow express your feelings for the others and WHAT YOU WOULD LIKE TO SHARE OF YOURSELF with each person.

In silence, think of the people in your group ... one at a time. Ask yourself, "If I could give each one a gift to express what these people mean to me, what would I like to give each one?" Take out your wallet and the things in your pockets and try to find something that symbolizes the *real* gift you would like to give to each person. For instance, you might choose for Dan a "fishing licence" because you would like to spend some more time with him and the licence is your "gift-token" that Dan can call on. For Mary, you might give a "blank cheque" that she can fill in. For Jim, you might give your "house key" to symbolize that your house is always open when he needs to talk to someone. DON'T GIVE OUT THE GIFTS YET. Just put them in front of you—one gift for each person. IF YOU CAN'T FIND THE GIFT IN YOUR WALLET, MAKE THE GIFT OUT OF PLASTICENE.

When everyone has chosen their gifts (after 5 minutes), one person sits in silence while the others give this person their gifts and explain the *meaning* and FEELINGS behind the gift. Then, ask the next person to sit in silence, and go around again, etc. ... until you have had a party for everyone in your group.

This game has tremendous potential for groups that know each other, BUT IT TAKES TIME. Allow at least 30 minutes for this game.

HOPE CHEST

Equipment: A small piece of cardboard for everyone, and a cup of crayons or coloured felt pens for each group.

This is similar to the Giving Game, but you sketch your hopes and dreams for each other on a piece of cardboard ... that can be kept as a "keepsake" from the group.

Give a piece of cardboard to everyone. Ask them to write their name on the top. Then, in silence, pass the cardboards around the group and allow everyone to draw or jot down the thing they would like to put in your Hope Chest.

When the cardboards have gone all the way around, one person sits in silence while the others explain what they drew and why. For instance, "I drew a 'horn of plenty' with lots of tender, loving care coming out of it, because I want you to have this for the rough times ahead."

When the night is over, the cardboards could be framed.

LYMAN COLEMAN

About the Author

I have written this Bible study program for myself. It may not help anyone else, but it is going to help me. I need a discipline in my spiritual growth—a structured program of Bible study, prayer, and a group to hold me accountable for my spiritual growth. This is what *Search the Scripture* is all about.

I need some people to belong to in the church. Not many, but a few people to share my life with. I need a way of saying hello to these people because I am naturally very shy . . . and a way to tell my story because a group cannot really love me until they know me . . . and a way to listen while the others in the group tell their story.

My problem is—I get lost in the bigness of the church . . . the big meetings . . . the big programs . . . even the big Bible study classes, where the teacher knows everything and does all the talking.

This is the reason I have written this program. I have written this program for myself and the people like me in the church who need to get together every week, study the Bible, and support one another in our spiritual struggles.

Cornbread, Mustard Greens and the Bible

I grew up in a family that read through the Bible together every year—from cover to cover, including the Notes. (Daddy thought the notes were inspired too.) We didn't have much money. In fact, I can still remember the hand-me-down clothes, the paper-sole shoes and the feed-sack shirts. But we had the Bible, a great church, and each other.

When I went off to college (Baylor University), I strayed a little from God, but I could not get away from the family roots. The cornbread, mustard greens, and Bible diet is hard to forget. Finally, the Navigators (a gung-ho, boot camp kind of approach to discipleship training) attracted me while I was floundering in psychology and philosophy. They taught me how to study the Bible for myself, and gave me a vision to make the church into small Bible study and growth groups.

While in seminary (Dallas and Biblical Seminary in New York), I specialized in small group technology and practiced on my Young Life kids when I was a club leader. Howard Hendricks (at Dallas Seminary) and Robert Traina (at Biblical and Asbury Seminary) showed me how to make Bible study exciting, especially for small groups.

Faith, Hope and a Shoestring

My brother, Robert, asked me to put together a program for discipleship groups in a local church. (His book, *Master Plan of Evangelism*, had caused a few pastors to rethink their role in the ministry as a "discipler" of people.) I decided to make this my project at New York University. Back in the 50's, there was not much written on this and I had to draw a lot of my ideas from secular programs—especially Alcoholics Anonymous.

In 1960, when I finished my program *Growth by Groups*, no one would publish it. So we published it ourselves, setting up shop in our spare bedroom. Only 100 churches responded to the program in the first three years and we had to sell our house twice to keep going.

In the meantime, I got involved in the early 60's in the Human Potential Movement and the dream of "humanizing" religious education with "sensitivity" and "group building." Most of the early Serendipity youth programs were written during those years.

In the 70's I felt the need in my own spiritual pilgrimage to integrate these two disciplines— disciplined Bible study and depth support groups—into a revised version of *Growth by Groups*. This is the background for this program.

A New Mousetrap for the 80's

I have integrated into this program three systems: (1) A system for training group leaders to start and shepherd Bible study groups, (2) A system for Bible study groups that lasts long enough for a group to develop into a depth community, (3) A system for reaching out to the kids and spouses of the Bible study group, and to build the larger group into an extended family.

In the first two units, I have combined Bible study with "group building," to give the group a chance to get acquainted before going deeper into Bible study. In the deeper Bible study units, I have provided Sharing Questions to keep the balance between Bible study and personal sharing. And running through the entire program is a series of covenants that provide entrances and exits into the group disciplines.

A Promised Land Somewhere

For myself, I continue to struggle to harmonize my old-fashioned spiritual heritage with contemporary needs in my own life and the life of the church. I feel like I have been sitting in the revolving Music Hall at Disneyland with the stage moving on in front of me every few years— and a new sound with each stage. On one stage is an 18th century chamber orchestra playing Bach—a little dull but secure and predictable. On the next stage, a Welsh choir is singing the grand old hymns of the faith that came out of the Wesleyan Revival—all in the minor key—heavy and dour (as only the Welsh can do it). On the next stage, a quartet from the deep South is wailing through a simple gospel chorus, pleading for sinners to come home. And on the last stage, Willie Nelson is crying out for authentic lifestyle in his own "outlaw," nonconformist style.

It has taken almost a lifetime to fully appreciate the rich heritage that I came from. In a real sense, the music from the four stages is starting to come together . . . the 17th century chamber music, the Wesleyan hymns, the Southern spirituals and the "outlaw" protests . . . into a new sound that seems more comfortable than any of these. I don't know whether there is a Promised Land in this world or not, but if there is, I think it will look something like a small, caring group where a few strugglers like me can belong and feel accepted—a real serendipity of sinners on our way to becoming the people of God.